Wilderness Next Door

John

ALONG THAT COAST

Along that coast the walker has his woods,
the small gold whistles and assault of birds,
the wind invisibly bright
and the black night pleasant.

Along that coast the fisherman may gather
glitter of fish and the encroaching weather,
out by the shoal where the freighters wade and glisten,
riding the hot lights home.

Out of the field that was fortress once
the lupines rise, meticulously blue:
the gunmounts, cold a generation now,
abandon outline, facing the contempt
and vast communication of the sea.

And there: that city. Where we fight
the battle with the robots every day.
That thinks itself a planet. Whose lords at night
have kept it burning
with a lidless fire —

city asleep in its wind-humming halls
that are lit from within and tremble with the sea —

But we are here to celebrate
that older brightness that surrounds us all:
these waves held up like incandescent chairs,
this radiance of grass on stone,
and flare of flowers —

with language, that was meant to make love evident
and by those images the eye was born to,
by which the lens and the emulsion make
defense and illustration of the day.

The camera knows the pattern of this place.
This is no rented house, it is your own:
is not synthetic, it is of whalebone made.
Be slow to judge the land before your face
that beats upon the brow with stubborn grace:

Whatever our invention may be worth
the power that is old in soil and air
is not suspended. We do well to care
for our good colleague, which is the body, earth.

Wilderness

San Francisco's

Next Door

By John Hart
Photographs by Robert Sena
Foreword by Cecil D. Andrus

PRESIDIO PRESS

San Rafael, California & London, England

Published by Presidio Press
of San Rafael, California, and London, England,
with editorial offices
at 1114 Irwin Street, San Rafael, California

Library of Congress Cataloging in Publication Data

Hart, John, 1948–
    San Francisco's wilderness next door.
    1. Golden Gate National Recreation Area, Calif.
    2. National parks and reserves — United States.
    I. Title.
F868.S156H37   979.4′61   79–1240
ISBN: 0–89141–042–2

Designed by Hal Lockwood

Composed by Lehmann Graphics

Printed in the United States of America
by Kingsport Press

To Lawrence Hart
and Jeanne McGahey

Contents

Foreword

THERE ARE MANY remarkable aspects of the parklands that radiate from the Golden Gate. Beaches, mountains, forests, historic ships, lighthouses and forts—the scenic, natural, and cultural resources of this relatively small area provide one of the richest and most varied collections of parkland in the world. Perhaps the most remarkable aspect is the fact that this rich array exists in the midst of one of the world's great cities.

San Francisco's "next door wilderness" did not come by accident. It is the result of citizen concern and dedication going back to the early years of this century. It is an outstanding example of how people who are willing to make the effort can work to preserve their cultural and natural heritage even as their city meets the challenges of economic growth.

In this poetic word and picture account, John Hart and Bob Sena describe this fascinating area and the movement to preserve its natural, historical, and recreational treasures. For residents of the Bay Area, this volume helps build appreciation for these treasures which they enjoy, and it serves as a reminder of their stewardship responsiblities for these treasures.

Perhaps the most important reason for telling this story, however, is that it can inspire other urban residents across America in their efforts to improve life in and around the cities.

Ultimately, one thing that will insure that this country's rich legacy of natural, historic, and recreational treasures will continue to be protected and enhanced is a deep sense of pride and ownership. That's what this is all about—that attitude evident in the people who saved and shaped San Francisco's wilderness next door.

CECIL D. ANDRUS
Secretary of the Interior
1979

Acknowledgments

ANYONE DOING A job of research grows quickly aware of the mass of misinformation abroad on almost any subject. To add to this mass—or even to miss a chance of subtracting from it—is an offense. My warm thanks go to the people who have aided my attempt to keep this story true.

First of all must come Bill Duddleson of the Department of the Interior, formerly an aide to Congressman Clem Miller, for his help and advice on many points but especially on the chapters concerned with Point Reyes National Seashore; Dr. Edgar Wayburn, Amy Meyer, and Robert Young of People for a Golden Gate National Recreation Area; John Langellier and his associates at the Presidio Army Museum; Doug Nadeau and Ron Treabess, co-leaders of the Point Reyes/GGNRA planning team; George Collins of Conservation Associates; Margot Patterson Doss; Peter Erickson, formerly of the Golden Gate Headlands Committee; Lawrence Hart; Jeanne McGahey; Larry Orman of People for Open Space; Salem Rice of the California Division of Mines; William Whalen, former General Manager of Bay Area National Parks, now Director of the National Park Service; and Chuck Williams of Friends of the Earth.

Much help came from the Golden Gate National Recreation Area staff: particularly John A. Martini, Stephen Heath, Ruth Kilday, John Sage, Bill Thomas, and General Superintendent Lynn Thompson. To these must be added John Adams, Gary Barbano, Gordon Chappell, and Woody Gray, all of the National Park Service (Western Region), and James R. Mills and Raymond I. Murray, Jr., of the Heritage Conservation and Recreation Service; also members of the state's Angel Island planning team and the volunteers at Kule Loklo, the reconstructed Miwok Indian village on Point Reyes.

The list, even after an arbitrary shortening, is long: Dave Ainley and the staff of the Point Reyes Bird Observatory; Jim Alexander; the staff of the Bancroft Library at the University of California (Berkeley); Representative Phillip Burton of San Francisco and his staff; Marion Hayes Cain of the Mountain Play Association; Carla Ehat; Representative James J. Florio of New Jersey; Marilyn Goudeau of the Miwok Archeological Preserve of Marin; Asa Hanamoto and Robert Sena of Royston, Hanamoto, Beck and Abey; Gladys Hansen of the San Francisco Public Library; Dot Hansen of the State Department of Parks and Recreation; John H. Jacobs (Executive Director, San Francisco Planning and Urban Research Association); Mrs. Thomas T. Kent; Marjorie Leland; Robert Lethbridge and Ray Murphy of the Marin Municipal Water District; Linda Massey of the Presidio public affairs staff; Ralph Moreno and the staff of the Mill Valley Public Library; Julie Manson; Mary New of the Tamalpais Conservation Club; Margaret Parkerson of the Marin County Free Library; Bob Raab of the Marin Conservation League; Rowan Rowntree; Peter Seligman of the Nature Conservancy; Sol Silver of the Marin County Planning Department; John Smail of the International Bird Rescue Research Center; Franklin Smith of Chamizal National Monument; Lt. Cmdr. L. B. Tyo of the U.S. Coast Guard; Sen. Harrison A. Williams, Jr., of New Jersey; and Peggy Woodring of the Metropolitan Transportation Commission.

An unpublished paper by Emanuel Raymond Lewis, "A History of San Francisco Harbor Defense Installations: Forts Baker, Barry, Cronkhite, and Funston," was invaluable in the preparation of Chapter 4.

In addition—and by no means as an automatic gesture—I would like to extend thanks to Joan Griffin and the staff of Presidio Press, who have made the preparation of this book an unusual pleasure.

Photographer's Note

WITHIN THE PHYSICAL constraints of the printed page and darkroom easel, the photographer must capture the essence of a place. I have approached the magnificence of the park recognizing the importance of every part in the makeup of the whole: noticing the direction the grass bends, the color of a leaf or a field, the special roundness of form or placement of edges, the yielding-molding relationship of surfshore.

I am never tempted to shoot every scene at 35 mm or wider. My contribution is an ability to recognize the fragment that will symbolize the whole, to fantasize a scene which summarizes my mood or emotion as I walk the park and then to find that scene.

The collection of photographs in this book represents the totality of the Golden Gate greenbelt. But *you* must go there to sense the stretch of sky, land and ocean which I have portrayed—to get your own lenses wet with surf—to feel the steepness of the headlands in your knees—to gasp at the surprises to be found around a bend or over a rise.

ROBERT SENA
1979

Part 1

The Wilderness Next Door

Greenbelt!

*F*ROM THE CITY of San Francisco, go north. Cross the rust-orange bridge above the wide, cold water of the Golden Gate. Travel a twisting road above the shore. Walk through a concrete tunnel in the hill: past the pit that was dug to house a gigantic coastal gun. Climb up a flight of wooden stairs — and there, from the top of the rise called Hill 129, what you have come to see is before you.

You are 900 feet above the water of the Golden Gate. Beyond, encrusting its peninsula like a deposit of white salt, is the city of San Francisco. Everything that might be dull or ugly in that city is, from this vantage, missing: rendered invisibly little: edited out. The buildings have become a texture, a stiff intricate fabric, spread over the humps and hollows. Though the mind knows better, the eye is deceived: old seamy San Francisco, urban crisis and all, looks like a trans-human city: a city without scars.

Turn now and face the north. In this direction you find no towers, no crust of streets and houses. Instead there is country, openness, horizon. Smooth hillsides slope down to ocean-facing bowls, rise again to higher and darker ridges. On a clear winter day you can make out forty miles of field and forest and brushland, dropping cleanly to the cliffs and coves of an almost uninhabited Pacific shore, before you lose the line of the coast in the far-off headlands.

Standing on this hill whose name is a number, you stand on a most unusual sort of boundary. For in this place, without any intervening ring of suburban clutter, the central city gives way all at once to a hinterland almost wild.

Golden Gate Bridge from Marin Headlands

Marin Headlands

To have such a meeting of opposite landscapes at all—that is unusual enough, near any city.

But to see a scene like this one, and know that what you see is permanent, that it will remain, that (in the dangerous neighborhood of an expanding urban area) it has been saved—this is nearly unheard of.

But here it has been achieved. Almost all the land you can see from this hilltop is either densely inhabited city or public, protected parkland. The green you see is going to stay green. There's no nervous need to "see it now, before they ruin it": fifty years from now, it will still be here. The valleys below are preserved, and so are the beaches and lagoons, and the sharp northern mountain called Tamalpais, and the far-off headlands, and more country you cannot see. And even at the south of the bridge, on the crowded urban shore, an extraordinary ring of parkland runs halfway round the twenty-mile coast of San Francisco.

Make no mistake: this is an unprecedented thing.

You might think that parks on this scale should be, even require to be, part of the makeup of any urban landscape. That a major city, a huge expanse of stone and steel and the wood of logged-off forests, should be coupled to a land-preserving park of national stature seems, on the face of it, merely in proportion. Each kind of grandeur augments the other. Standing on the windy headland over the Golden Gate, looking from the green or tawny land across to the pale city, it is easy to fall into this way of thinking. Of course this land is a park. What else would it be?

4

But there seems to be a social law which causes the great city to destroy what is most interesting about its landscape. The bank of the river becomes a zone of blight. The lakeshore is divided between industry and the houses of the very rich. The magnificent view is shut out by the apartment block. Even the small town, admired for its charming location among orchards, is driven to pave and consume its own valuable setting.

And so we have built cities in which the feeling of being in any definable place whatsoever is lost: not single towns but endless agglomerations of towns, spreading across whole counties and threatening to dominate the landscapes of whole states.

The growing city-mass seldom leaves much green land within its huge perimeter. The urban planners of the nineteenth century set aside Central Park and Golden Gate Park; their successors in today's vaster metropolises are doing less well. Away from the city—a long way away—the nation has preserved splendid park and forest lands; but these in most cases are distant even from the suburbs and are almost useless to people who live in core cities and own no cars.

Our world has pulled apart into unsatisfactory halves: the urban expanses—which people may claim to dislike, but where, willy-nilly, they work and live—and the far-off wilderness and recreational lands, reachable only at large expense in money and in time.

It should not be so.

It approaches insanity that it should be so.

Estero de Limantour, Point Reyes

In many places, in many ways, people are trying to prevent it from being so: trying, at least, to rescue fragments of urban parks and greenbelts that might have been.

But if there is one place where success in that effort can be called major, it is here, at San Francisco. Around the Golden Gate a park has been built that would be magnificent anywhere, but whose existence, so near to the great city, seems scarcely credible: a wilderness next door.

THE GREENBELT BEGINS near the business center of San Francisco, almost at the base of office towers. A narrow coastal strip, it curves along the shore of San Francisco Bay, west to the Golden Gate. There the arc of public land turns south and follows the cliffs and dunes of the city's ocean shore.

The bulkier part of the park, cut off by water, begins with the Headlands north of the Golden Gate. For sixty miles it continues on that coast, to end at the foggy bluffs of the Point Reyes Peninsula. This is no beachside strip but a broad band of parkland, never less than several miles wide.

Most parks in America on this scale are, so to speak, inherited: they are fragments of the original public domain. Nobody had to buy them. But here, in the Golden Gate greenbelt, nearly all the land was once private: open for development: up for grabs. Such a sweep of publicly owned land could only have been assembled—so it would seem—by a long, persistent, well-directed campaign.

And yet—a curious fact—there was never a grand design. There were, instead, over the space of a hundred years, a hundred small designs. The park was put together piece by isolated piece. Hardly anyone dared to think, until the very end, that the pieces would finally fuse. Slowly, irregularly, yet in the long run steadily, the work of preservation went on.

San Francisco was lucky—lucky almost past belief. Its greenbelt grew nearly as inexorably as its suburbs did. At almost every point of decision— and there were many—the choice was made for preservation. The long chain of necessary events could have failed at any link; always, somehow, it held. And when, in the early 1970s, people began to see the importance of saving the greenbelt completely, filling in the gaps that still remained, this was a possible thing.

Can we do for other American cities what was done for San Francisco and its region? Attempts are being made in Los Angeles, New Orleans, Atlanta, and New York. Other cities will follow. Each time—this we can count on—the achievement will be more difficult. It will cost more money for the same result; it will take more ingenuity, more compromise.

But because this Golden Gate greenbelt was completed, because it is there and so assertively splendid, it becomes the model to which other great park projects near cities are compared.

Its creation changed the rules.

Anatomy of a Greenbelt

*Y*OU WILL SEE few maps that show the Golden Gate greenbelt as the single thing it is. Though it is almost all in public ownership, it is not entirely in *one* public ownership. It is a jigsaw puzzle of lands under different managements.

By far the largest part is in two federal parks: the Golden Gate National Recreation Area in San Francisco and southern Marin and, farther north, Point Reyes National Seashore. Other pieces of the puzzle are state parks: Mount Tamalpais, Tomales Bay, Samuel Taylor, Angel Island. Others still are watershed lands controlled by a local district. Some sections have been in protected ownership for fifty years; others were not taken out of the reach of private development till the late 1970s. Here and there a piece is owned by a private organization with preservation in mind.

The one long gap in the greenbelt is a gap in the land itself: the Golden Gate, entry into one of the world's finest harbors. The Gate divides the park into its larger and wilder portion, north of the water, and its smaller but more accessible part, on the shores of San Francisco to the south. The link—the big rust-colored pin—is the Golden Gate Bridge. This is one of the few major highway bridges that have pedestrian walkways. For the traveler on foot, as well as for the driver or bus passenger, this is a link and not a barrier.

*O*NLY ABOUT TWO percent of the greenbelt actually lies inside San Francisco. It is quite arguably the most important two percent. The park gives the city a thin green rim: an open coast that includes all but a few hundred yards of

The San Francisco Side

Baker Beach and Lands End

the city's ocean shore and about a quarter of its frontage on the quieter water of San Francisco Bay. (This coastal strip is in itself a remarkable achievement. Neither on Manhattan nor in park-rich Washington, D.C., will you find so long an open shore. The one city that has managed something comparable is Chicago.) These are the lands that bring the greenbelt right into the population center—you can step into the park from a cable car.

The San Francisco lands now combined in the Golden Gate National Recreation Area were formerly many things: city parks, state parks, private tourist attractions. But the most important sections belonged for a hundred years to the army. Though the army kept much of its territory off-limits to the public, it preserved it, as no other agency could have done, from development. Now that this land is open, linking the other zones of public ownership, San Franciscans are suddenly aware of what they have: a whole that is startlingly greater than the sum of its parts.

The eastern entry to the greenbelt is *Aquatic Park,* a bayfront green next to Fisherman's Wharf and Ghirardelli Square. There are fishing and swimming behind a curving pier. Wooden ships, museum-pieces, float on the water. This is to be the "front door" of the Golden Gate National Recreation Area—the entry point.

To the west rises *Fort Mason,* one of the old military properties: a wooded bluff with cypresses and clusters of historic buildings. A few hundred feet of natural bay shoreline (a rarity) curve below.

Next is the *San Francisco Marina,* still in city care: two yacht harbors, a seawall, a long green rectangle of lawn. Then follows the less-manicured but sandier shoreline known as *Crissy Field.* This two-mile strip of beaches and flat uplands was taken, for the park, from the big army base just inland, the famous Presidio.

At its western end the field narrows to *Fort Point,* the tip of San Francisco and the anchorage of the Golden Gate Bridge. Under the bridge is the fort itself, a brick and granite gun-castle that has been there a hundred years.

At Fort Point the coast turns south; the park now has an ocean surf. The first long stretch is *Baker Beach,* the ocean shore of the Presidio, backed by cliffs and woods of cypress and pine. South of this beach the coastal greenbelt is interrupted for the first and only time: private houses have been permitted to press right to the cliff-edge. But shortly the public shoreline resumes with *Lands End.* This is the northwest corner of the city. Inland the scene is quiet: a golf course, woods, old fortifications in the one-time military enclave called *Fort Miley.* A couple of big buildings—a hospital, a museum—rise out of the green. But on the sea, rugged and overgrown cliffs drop to dangerous surf. Near the water are the ruins of the old *Sutro Baths* and, beside them, one of San Francisco's most famous landmarks: the *Cliff House.* It belongs to the Park Service now. *Seal Rocks,* a wildlife refuge, break the blue swells a few hundred yards offshore.

South of Lands End the coast changes character, becoming low and sandy. Here, bordered by highway, runs *Ocean Beach,* long, narrow and weather-swept. After three miles it rises in crumbling sandstone cliffs to a high dune-covered plateau. This is old *Fort Funston,* another artillery base turned recreational area, and the last of the connected parks on San Francisco's shore.

The Islands

NONE OF THE Golden Gate greenbelt is far from salt water, but some of it is surrounded by water: the islands, Angel and Alcatraz. Just inside the Gate, a mile and one-half apart, they were set aside early for bay defense. They make an odd pair.

Alcatraz (the name is from the Spanish word for "pelicans") lies a mile offshore from Aquatic Park. It began as a fort and went through several uses before it became what it will always be in the public mind: the prison of prisons. Grim buildings, grimmer ruins cover most of it. Some people want it leveled to bare rock; others want some sort of monument, a Statue to Peace perhaps, or a western Statue of Liberty. But even as it is, the island is a monument.

Gentler, if not without grim spots in its history, is *Angel Island,* nearby to the north. Angel is broad and soft, a green square mile rising to a central mountain. After the army lost interest in the island, the state acquired it for a park. Only a few hundred yards of deep water separate the place from the populated bay shore of Marin.

Marin Headlands

The Marin Side   I*F IT WERE* not for the army's immovable occupancy, the steep dark Headlands of Marin would certainly, by now, be covered with houses: houses for the discriminating rich who would pay for one of the loveliest views in the world. But because of the army, the land just north of the Golden Gate (though it shows an archeology of old gunmounts) is essentially empty. This is the unforgettable border: the spot where the city and the open land adjoin like nations in a hard-won, stable peace.

North of their first sharp wall against the Golden Gate the *Marin Headlands* continue high for miles; but a west-facing valley hollows them. You reach this valley by tunnel and can follow it out to a fine Pacific beach. In the north branch of the valley (not controlled by the army) ground was actually once broken for what was to be a city of 18,000 people. How that project arose, and how after all it was halted, is told in Chapter 7.

Upcoast the Headlands mountain block ends suddenly at *Tennessee Valley,* a long depression running east and west between the ocean and the bay. North again the coastal hills gather themselves by stages into the dark mass of *Mount Tamalpais,* the highest land in the greenbelt.

The mountain was one of the first areas in the greenbelt region to draw the concern of conservationists. Most of the west side of the massif is now a state park. At the mountain's base is a shoreline so rugged that, even in this region of stark coasts, it has a special vivid wildness.

North of its main summits Tamalpais runs out in a long, slowly subsiding range called Bolinas Ridge. East of the ridge, inland, lies the forest-bound valley of Lagunitas Creek; its watershed belongs to the Marin Municipal Water District. To the west you would expect the ridge to drop to salt water. It doesn't. Instead there is a pastoral lowland and beyond it, pushing far west of the general line of this coast, a most remarkable peninsula.

The intervening lowland, the *Olema Valley,* is itself a landscape of intriguing history. It marks the course of the San Andreas Fault, the great slipjoint in the earth that moved in 1906 and shook San Francisco down. At both ends of the valley, south and north, the sea has flooded into it, forming narrow bays. Bolinas Lagoon is the southern embayment; Tomales Bay, much larger, is the northern. Between them they make *Point Reyes,* west of the faultline, halfway an island.

Punta de Los Reyes, the Spanish explorers named the peninsula: the Point of the Three Kings. Though you can see it from San Francisco, Point Reyes has always seemed remote and separate. It has, indeed, an island feeling. Half a century after conservationists had gotten to work on Tamalpais they recognized, barely in time, the value of Point Reyes: the forests, the lakes, the beaches; the rocky coves with rookeries of seals; the tidepools with their soft florid animals; the mudflats where the tall stiff birds stand up from their reflections on the water.

In 1962 Congress created Point Reyes National Seashore. Most of the peninsula is within its boundaries. The Seashore contains almost half the acreage of the completed greenbelt, much of its finest scenery, its most abundant wildlife, and all of its formally designated roadless wilderness. Though some of this land is wild only by contrast with developed areas, it grows more natural with every day that it is left alone. In a few years there will be wilderness here, not by courtesy of law or metaphor, but in plain fact.

Point Reyes is the climax. Or rather it is one of the two climaxes: one of the two poles between which all the landscapes of the greenbelt extend. Here is resurgent wilderness: there, across valley and mountain and salt water, is the city. Wherever you go in the greenbelt you are aware of both. Each, by being completely what it is, gives value to the other, and to all the varied country in between.

Part 2
The Saving

The Park That
Almost Wasn't

*L*OOKING BACK OVER the years it seems incredible that the Golden
Gate greenbelt should survive, so nearly intact, so close to the center
of the metropolitan area. You can state the reasons that explain its
survival: the military importance of the Golden Gate; the ruggedness of coastal
hills that at first made development difficult; the presence, from the turn of the
century, of a rambunctious local conservation movement. But the logical
explanations do not satisfy. The achievement required something less easily
accounted for: consistent and unreasonable luck. With a few exceptions, the
breaks, when it counted most, went the right way.

It is a long, eventful, odd, and admirable story, the story of the saving.
Four key dates stand out.

The first is 1851, when President Millard Fillmore signed the proclama-
tion creating the Presidio Military Reservation in San Francisco and the Lime
Point Reservation across the water in the Headlands.

The second great year is 1903, when William Kent of Kentfield in Marin
County began a long and stubborn campaign for the preservation of Mount
Tamalpais. The civic leader (later congressman) wanted a national park on the
mountain, settled instead for a state park, a minor national monument, and a
park-like municipal watershed; to all he gave, lavishly, his own land. His work
and his gifts made Tamalpais the second nucleus of public land within the
future greenbelt.

The third key date is 1958, when the National Park Service released a
report calling for the creation of Point Reyes National Seashore: "a combination of scenic, recreation, and biologic interests that can be found nowhere else
in this country as near to a large center of population."

And the fourth was 1970, when a debate over what to do with Alcatraz Island grew by stages into a citizen campaign for a new federal park to fill the gaps among the military holdings, Tamalpais, and Point Reyes, and to be called the Golden Gate National Recreation Area.

These dates have to do with the positive achievements: the acts of preservation. Less remembered but no less necessary were the negative victories: the acts of obstructionism, if you like, that accomplished nothing in themselves but merely kept the possibilities open.

We owe the park to the people who, after World War II, fought to prevent the disposal of the military lands to private use.

We owe it to the people who turned out by the hundreds in the 1960s to persuade the state not to build freeways: the one that would have covered the San Francisco waterfront from Fort Mason to Fort Point, the one that would have cut its massive way into western Marin, the one that would have ridden the crest of Bolinas Ridge.

We owe it to the people who spent years resisting various plans to civilize Bolinas Lagoon at the foot of Mount Tamalpais: plans for marinas, a racetrack, an urban-scale sewer project.

And we owe it to that stubborn group, a minority even among conservationists, who refused to accept the grand-scale development that almost occupied the Headlands — who continued, when hope seemed gone, to oppose Marincello.

The stories are endless. Only a very few of them are told in this book. But if even one of them were missing from the true and untold history, the balance of the events might have been very different. The greenbelt we have today might be much less — or might not exist at all.

SIR FRANCIS DRAKE

FOUR HUNDRED YEARS ago, in the summer of 1579, Sir Francis Drake was off these coasts and on the run. The first Englishman to penetrate the Spanish Pacific, he had just spent six months raiding Spain's New World empire; he had taken, in just one of many piracies, twenty-six tons of silver. He had been north to Oregon, looking for the legendary Straits of Anian—"a nearer cut and passage home." Not finding such an escape, he knew that his only way back to England was west across the Pacific—a course that would make his *Golden Hinde* the second ship (Magellan's was the first) to sail around the world.

But the *Golden Hinde,* heavy with loot and leaking badly, was in no shape for such a voyage. Drake now needed a certain kind of harbor—small, hospitable, sheltered both from weather and from hostile observation. There the vessel would be careened: tipped dangerously over, almost to capsizing, first on one side, then on the other, while the crew cleaned and repaired the exposed sections of hull.

On June 17, 1579, Drake found his harbor. He built a fort, began repairs on his ship, and awed the local Indians. Later they crowned him (or so he took the honor) with a cap of feathers and with necklaces of bone. He complained of the fog and the barren landscape at the shore. He hiked "up into the land" and found that country greener. He set up, "on a greate and firme post," a plate of brass claiming all North America, north of the Spanish lands, for Queen Elizabeth. On July 23 he reembarked. After a stop for sea-bird eggs at certain offshore islands, he sailed on west, leaving behind him questions not yet answered and perhaps unanswerable.

Where was it, exactly, that he landed? What landscape did he have before him when he named the country a new England: *Nova Albion?*

Almost certainly, it was somewhere in Marin County. The latitude is correct. Anthropologists say that his Indians could only have been the Coast Miwoks, who lived in a rather narrow region north of the Golden Gate. On his way to harbor he passed certain high white cliffs that reminded him of the southern English coast: in all California there is only one set of seacliffs that meet that description, and those are at Point Reyes. The seabird egg islands can only be the Farallones.

So this is the region in which he landed, but we can only guess at the exact spot. And for two hundred years scholars and zealous amateurs have been struggling to pin down that grand historic site.

Drake kept an illustrated log that would have answered every question. But this, with all the rest of the original record, he gave to Queen Elizabeth in 1580. The Queen suppressed the information and may have destroyed it. England and Spain, though headed for war, were technically at peace; Drake's highly irregular raid—an "undercover operation"—was not for public knowledge. Only in 1588, after war had come, was the "Top Secret" stamp taken off the story. Before he could write his own account, Sir Francis Drake died at sea.

Thus we are left with secondhand and lesser sources. One important piece of evidence is a map of Drake's landing drawn by the Dutch cartographer Hondius in 1595. But enough time had elapsed—fifteen years—to blur the details that would distinguish one site plainly from another. The source scholars cite most often is a book called *The World Encompassed,* which purports to be based on the journal of Drake's chaplain, Francis Fletcher. This book, however, did not appear until 1628—fifty years after the voyage!

The scholars (to give them credit) have made the most of what they have. They have analyzed every bit of information from Fletcher's account and others: sailing times, descriptions of vegetation, comments on climate, wind, and topography. They have trundled up and down the California coast, holding the Hondius map at curious angles against every possible cove or bay. Currently the controversy has narrowed to three likely sites.

One authority holds that Drake was the discoverer of San Francisco Bay. Two hundred years before the Spanish found it, he may have sailed through the Golden Gate and anchored not far from Angel Island. From that island he drew the sketch that became the Hondius map.

A second authority puts Drake at Bolinas Lagoon. The pioneer of this theory insists that he has found, under the banks of an old pond, the traces of Drake's stockade.

The third authority—the most widely accepted one—places the *Golden Hinde* at a cove, now filled with silt, just inside the mouth of Drakes Estero at Point Reyes. Much of what we read in *The World Encompassed*—the complaint of perpetual fog, the seeming barrenness of the coast, the greenness of the inland region— seems to fit this site more naturally than any other.

Sir Francis Drake and the Miwoks. From Frank Soulé, Annals of San Francisco *(New York, 1855).*

All authorities profess absolute certainty. All, of course, are guessing.

Are there no traces on, or in, the land? At Bolinas Lagoon, diggers have found remnants of old earthworks that might go back to the sixteenth century. There are also possible traces at Drakes Estero — yet the evidence is thin at both places.

On Point Reyes, exotic artifacts of the proper period have turned up in Indian middens. Unfortunately, a Spanish galleon was wrecked off the Point a decade after Drake departed, so none of the finds can be traced with certainty to him.

In 1977 an Elizabethan sixpence was found on the opposite side of Marin County, near the shore of San Francisco Bay. If it came from the *Golden Hinde,* as one researcher believes, the coin could have been picked up at any of the rival landing sites.

What about the most famous artifact of all — the plate of brass that Drake set up on his "greate and firme post" in the new land of Albion?

In 1936 a plate with the proper inscription was found on the east shore of Marin. But, like the sixpence, the plate had traveled. It neither proved nor disproved any case. Instead it added a new question: Was this Drake's plate or a brilliant forgery? For years the plate was thought to be genuine. Recently, however, metallurgists have taken a hard second look. Their verdict: the plate is probably made of modern metal, and is a fake.

The central mystery does not diminish. Maybe it never will.

Four hundred years is a long time.

The Forts

*T*HERE WAS A city, and there was a harbor.

The city, at first, was nothing much: a gaggle of huts: an impoverished pueblo on the ill-supplied northern limit of the Spanish Empire in the New World. But San Francisco Bay was something marvelous: huge and sheltered, easily guarded, big enough (as has so often been said) to float all the navies of the nations of the world. Military men saw in the bay the key to the West Coast. "There is not another *good* harbor," one of them wrote, "between Cape Horn and the Bering Straits."

Who could doubt that it needed defending?

The Spanish started it. In 1776 they laid out, near the Golden Gate, their northernmost Presidio. In 1794 they built, on a steep white bluff commanding the wide strait, a fortress called the *Castillo de San Joaquin.* And on the point we now know as Fort Mason, they installed another nest of cannon: *Batería de Yerba Buena.*

But the Spanish hold on upper California, never very firm, was already slipping away. Neither the Spanish nor their Mexican successors were able to complete the defenses they planned. By 1846, in fact, the original garrisons had been moved elsewhere. It was an unoccupied *Castillo* that John C. Frémont captured during the Bear Flag Revolt; the guns he spiked were probably already useless.

The new American owners wanted no such vulnerability. At once they set the engineers to work on grandiose plans for fortification. In 1850, on November 1, President Millard Fillmore signed an executive order that already contained the hidden possibility of the Golden Gate greenbelt of today.

Barbettes, Fort Point

He set aside, "for public purposes," both coasts of the Golden Gate—the old San Francisco Presidio (with its eastern satellite, Fort Mason) and the steep-fronted, still-wild Headlands of Marin.

Some of this land was private and hard to acquire. When the owner of the Headlands asked $200,000—a huge price for the time—Congress fumed. "This is an enormous fraud," said Senator David Broderick. "To pay $200,000 for 2,300 or 23,000 acres of barren land shall never receive my sanction." But in the end the essential lands on both sides of the water, and Alcatraz and Angel Islands as well, were in federal hands.

No power in the country, besides the military, could have secured these lands. No power, besides the military, would have troubled to keep them free of housing and commerce. And so it is to the army that we owe the complete uniqueness of the Golden Gate greenbelt: that it is not merely a great park *near* a city, but a great park *adjoining* a city, overlapping a city.

The Armaments

THE PLAN OF 1850 showed two lines of defense: an inner rank of guns, at Fort Mason and on Alcatraz and Angel Islands; and an outer line, at the Golden Gate itself. Soon ninety cannon had been put on Alcatraz; but the planners' focus was Fort Point, the site of the Spanish *Castillo*. "I look upon this point," wrote Joseph K. F. Mansfield in a survey of western defenses, "as the key to the whole Pacific Coast in a military point of view, and it should receive untiring exertion."

It did. The original vertical white cliff (the Spanish *cantil blanco*) was leveled almost to waterline. On the new low platform the engineers built the elegant brick and granite blockhouse that you see today, under the humming deck of the Golden Gate Bridge. With its three long tiers of gunports, its rooftop barbettes, its seven-foot-thick walls, and its splendid position on the Gate, the fort was thought to be impregnable. When it first got its guns in 1861, it probably was.

To hold the Golden Gate, however, Fort Point required a twin: a similar castle across the water, at Lime Point on the Headlands. To make room for the structure on those more precipitous slopes, a great mass of rock would have to be blasted away. In 1868 and 1869, 171,000 cubic yards of Lime Point chert were dynamited into the harbor opening. Observers were delighted "at the scale of these operations."

But before the demolition could go further (and this was only the beginning) something happened that would occur at least twice more in the story of the harbor forts. In April 1869 the authorities issued a verdict that made the enterprise meaningless. The whole 1850 plan of defense—once ultramodern, complete, the best in the world—was hopelessly out of date.

Back when Millard Fillmore had set the forts aside, the standard cannon used round shot and could carry about two miles—and could certainly not penetrate stout brick walls. An installation like Fort Point could lay down its barrage without much fear of the returning fire.

By the end of the Civil War, guns had changed. Armorers had started building cannon that used a cylindrical shell—the familiar "bullet shape"— and had a rifled barrel, scored inside with spiral lines, to give the projectile a stabilizing spin. The new guns could shoot much farther than the old, about ten miles, and no brick wall, however thick, was a defense against them.

One answer to the threat was armor plating. The engineers loved the idea. Plans were offered in the 1860s (and after) that would have made the Golden Gate an almost medieval landscape. Imagine two enormous revolving armored turrets, one each at Fort Point and Lime Point, with a third such tower rising from a shoal in the water between them . . . imagine, strung across the Gate, lifted by winches to let friendly traffic through, a stupendous iron chain.

But such notions were expensive, and Congress, in the years just after the Civil War, was not in a spending mood. In fact very little work of any kind was done on the Golden Gate forts during this period. The few new emplacements that were built were protected, not by steel, but by mounds of earth. It was just as well. By the time the military budget began to swell once more, the tools of war had changed again.

Fort Point and the Golden Gate. From Resources of California *(San Francisco, 1884).*

The Busy Years THE INNOVATIONS THIS time were subtler. Gun barrels were stronger—built up in layers, onion-fashion. Slow-burning "smokeless" powders propelled missiles faster, yet put less stress on the gun. Ammunition now could be loaded into the breech, not the muzzle. Even the mounts of the guns were changing: the latest thing was the "disappearing carriage," on which the gun could sink out of danger between firings. The new order was announced in 1885 by President Grover Cleveland's Endicott Board. The board offered a plan for a whole new system of national coastal defenses, estimated, even then, to cost $126 million.

The resulting new armament plan for San Francisco Bay, pushed forward by the Spanish-American War, was carried out more completely than any similar scheme before or after. Most of the massive concrete emplacements you see today around the Golden Gate belong to the Endicott generation. The nests are everywhere: on Angel Island, at Fort Mason, on the two coasts of the Presidio, and throughout the Headlands.

With increasing range, the center of the system shifted toward the sea. For the first time, land was purchased outside the original reservations: at Fort Miley near Lands End in San Francisco and, three miles farther south, at Fort Funston.

Tom Killion

The gunners, at their increasingly capable machines, needed better estimates of range. These they derived by triangulation, comparing compass bearings taken on their targets from widely separated coastal points. As the ranges of the guns grew still longer, the outlying spotter stations had to be built farther and farther away from the actual emplacements; at the end they were scattered from the tip of Point Reyes on the north to Half Moon Bay on the south. You can see them now in clifftop fields, tiny thick-walled dugouts. You can climb down into them and look through narrow slits at the horizon over which no enemy ship ever came.

By 1914 the system was considered complete. Almost needless to say, it was also substantially obsolete. In 1912 Britain had floated the first of its Dreadnought-class battleships, so massively armed that conventional coastal forts could not repel them. In 1915, after the inevitable review, came the inevitable government report—and the inevitable new plan.

THE NEW SCHEME called for the largest coastal defense guns that would ever be built. Sixteen inches in the bore, they could send projectiles weighing more than a ton a distance of twenty-eight miles. Barrel and carriage together weighed one million pounds.

The Last of the Guns

There was a twenty-year lag between the formulation of these plans and their execution. World War I did not threaten the West Coast, and the 1920s were a slack period for military spending. But in 1935, when the Japanese refused to renew the naval arms limitation pact of 1922, the defense of San Francisco became a national order of business. The first of the coastal sixteen-inchers—the national prototype—went into Battery Davis at Fort Funston in 1940. Next Battery Townsley, at Tennessee Point in the Headlands, was built and armed. Since the threat of attack from the air was by now real, these last and largest of the Golden Gate emplacements are buried in earth, concrete, and steel.

The very last complex to be built was the one that hollows out Hill 129, 900 feet above the Golden Gate. (It is here that visitors by the thousands walk through the ridge in the battery's tunnels and climb stairs to the hilltop lookout—not to spot enemy vessels, but to look at the city, the greenbelt, and the sea.) But Hill 129, hollowed and shaped and fortified, never received its pair of guns. In 1943 this project—like the Lime Point undertaking seventy-five years earlier—was canceled, incomplete.

This time it was no mere change in artillery styles that caused the work to stop, not just a certain barrel or carriage design that was obsolete. The end had come for the whole concept of fixed-gun coastal defense. The edge of the continent, from the military point of view, had moved up, and out, and away. For a time the Nike anti-airplane missiles and their humped, white radar domes succeeded the guns in the Headlands and at Fort Funston. Then these too were gone. Outlying buildings, boarded up against the weather, turned slowly gray. The empty gunmounts faced the empty sea.

IF THE GOVERNMENT no longer needed the land for coastal defense, did it need the land at all? The question was not entirely novel. Back before the Spanish-American War there had been recurrent talk of declaring some acreage surplus and selling it off—even, on one occasion, of making the Presidio a city park. Now the talk began again, but the park idea was slow to reemerge.

Who Gets the Land?

In 1945 President Truman offered the Presidio to the United Nations for its headquarters. (Angel Island was mentioned, too.) The army was greatly relieved when the world organization chose New York instead. But the UN offer made the historic military enclave seem expendable. Backed by politicians and the press, the city of San Francisco promoted a plan to cover the green slopes of the Presidio with housing: high-rise buildings on the bluffs, 75,000 single-family houses on bay fill and in the interior. Though the army resisted successfully, it was not until the early 1960s that the city gave up its hope of urbanizing the shore of the Golden Gate.

By that time peripheral fragments of the old forts complex were actually being disposed of. In 1960 a parcel of the Headlands was released. It took a lively campaign by conservationists in Congress and at home to prevent the Eisenhower administration from passing the land directly to developers. The property, one high official remarked, was "too valuable for park purposes." Much the same thing happened at Fort Funston, this threat also being turned aside.

Some curious proposals to sell or trade military land in order to rescue struggling park projects elsewhere also arose. Funston was twice considered for such bargains — once as a trade for land at Lake Tahoe, once for a parcel in Point Reyes National Seashore. (*That* would have been a strange transaction, robbing one end of the future greenbelt to save the other!)

After a time the sell-off attempts grew rarer, but another kind of pressure grew. Government is itself a builder, and here, in the middle of a metropolitan area, was an unmatched stock of unoccupied low-cost land. It seemed at times that every agency with a building to put up proposed to erect it here: federal and municipal archives, schools, warehouses, even jails. The state, for its part, wanted to route a freeway through Fort Mason and Crissy Field. And on the Presidio, the army itself had a major construction program. When San Franciscans resisted Presidio building, pressure shifted to the Marin forts; an ad hoc organization, Headlands, Inc., arose to defend them.

Many accounts could be given of debates, of narrow escapes, of reprieves and also of losses. But, one by one, the crises passed. The forts stayed more or less intact. And, at last, conservationists, tired of being always in the opposition, found a proposal they could wholeheartedly work for: the creation, out of the old forts, of the Golden Gate National Recreation Area.

Today, of some 6,400 acres in the original forts, about 4,800 belong to the greenbelt. A few small enclaves are still army-held, and so is one very large one — the inland region of the Presidio. Some army authorities say that the Presidio will always be needed as the headquarters of the Sixth Army and for other military tenants. But in 1978 the talk had turned once more to closure. Under the Recreation Area law, any lands released from the base will go, without further debate, to the park. It seems inevitable that some day essentially all of the army's acreage will have been transferred.

When President Fillmore reserved the Golden Gate forts, he did not specify "defense" as the reason, but only "public purposes." It is hard to refrain from reading his ambiguity as a promise, now fulfilled. Public purposes can change, and have.

THE GOLDEN GATE country is not kind to its old emplacements. There is too much salt in the air, and too much moisture. Already the fortifications seem older than they are. They have an outworn, prehistoric look: as if somehow miraculously we had freed ourselves from the dangers and fears and dilemmas that caused us to make them: as if we had solved the intractable problem of war.

Here is the cavern of Battery Davis, under its huge protective casemate, hollowing a sand dune at Fort Funston, long streaks of orange rust on its concrete walls. The little green forest back of Kirby Cove, where emplacements of three generations overlap. Battery Townsley on Tennessee Point, in whose dark tunnels I trespassed as a boy. Platforms. Hollows. Earthworks. Stairs. Piles of dull spherical archaic shot. The curious spotters' huts, clumsily camouflaged with sod and stones.

Some sightseers can look at the remainders and tell themselves that these are not impressive, not even interesting; that only a cruel waste is represented here; that there is nothing to catch the mind in the flags and rituals of the old Presidio. Others, of different political leaning, admire the old armaments as wholeheartedly as they admire the new, and do not acknowledge the melancholy that one feels in these places, the slight but ineradicable sadness.

In truth both are real, both the glamour and the sadness, both the waste and the sometimes terrible pressure of need. Who can forget, surveying this history, that we seem always to have been in one arms race or another—that every peacetime we have known so far has been an interlude only, an *entre-deux-guerres?*

Out of it all, we get a strange inheritance: a park that is the equal of the harbor and the city and is, indeed, one of the remarkable things of the world.

Mount Tamalpais

A PARK NEEDS A mountain. Though the Golden Gate greenbelt has nothing like real high country, it does have its dominant peak—a summit with a reputation out of all proportion to its size—perhaps the most hiked-over, written-about hill in the western United States: Mount Tamalpais.

The peak is hardly huge—2,604 feet, half a vertical mile—but it rises almost without foothills from coastal beaches, bayside flats, and deep interior canyons. Simple, stark, and massive, it looks higher than it is. An early journalist wrote of it: "It stands in Marin County, or rather, it is Marin County; for take away Tamalpais and what is left hardly fills a wheelbarrow." The name, from the Miwok Indian language, means Bay Country Mountain or West Hill.

Nine miles north of the Golden Gate, it is the only California peak of any size so close to a sea-level gap in the coastal ranges; this gives it a damp and complicated weather. Even without the coastal fogs that moisten its lower slopes in summer (typically the peak remains in sunlight above them), Tamalpais is high enough to put an eddy into the rainfall charts: in a reversal of the general trend, it is wetter than lands to the north. Kentfield, at the mountain's eastern foot, has an annual average rainfall of forty-six inches, double the quota of places set among lower hills.

The walkers on the mountain—they come by the tens of thousands— find the landscape always changing. The vegetation is immensely varied, from deep redwood canyons to hot sunny chaparral to fog-blown grasslands over against the horizon of salt water. When you're in the shade of the conifers,

they seem likely to go on forever; but five minutes later you will be walking in an open meadow with running springs, or on a serpentine barren with bear grass and unfamiliar flowers. The views out from the mountain shift almost as quickly: now ocean, now bay, now lake, now suburb and city. It used to be said that, from the top on a clear day, you could see one-third of the area of California. This seems unlikely, but certainly most of the Bay Area is at your feet.

*The Crookedest
Railroad*

MOUNT TAMALPAIS BEGAN to be climbed and celebrated very early. Even in the 1880s, when transportation was slow, people apparently thought it rather special to have this recreational area so close to where they lived. "The ascent is but an easy pleasure-ride from San Rafael, between the hours of breakfast and supper," wrote a historian in 1880. "Far grander and higher [is] the Yosemite's white dome," a local poet admitted, "but less dear to my heart, because farther from home!" Tamalpais attracted poetry, most of it bad, from the beginning.

The 1880 historian had one complaint about the mountain: it was over-wild. "Looking up Mount Tamalpais from any point in this valley, its slopes present no evidence to the eye of the invading march of improvement . . . it would be the last place to go to find the trophies of cunning workmanship, or to see a grand achievement of labor and engineering skill."

That, however, was to change. In 1896, in the space of just a few months, there was created an up-to-date way to the top: the Mill Valley and Mount Tamalpais Scenic Railroad. The starting point, near sea level at the mountain's eastern base, was less than two miles from the summit. To make the climb at a reasonable grade, engineers laid out an elaborate course more than eight miles long. It had 281 curves, which (it was said) would add up to forty-two complete circles. The longest straight section was 413 feet. Soon the line came to be called "The Crookedest Railroad in the World."

It was also one of the most celebrated. In the first year it carried 23,000 people to the summit. Railroad publicity, lavish and international, compared the Tamalpais line to similar routes in the Alps. Whole conventions traveled up the mountain, and Mrs. Teddy Roosevelt spent several weeks at the luxurious summit hotel. One writer called the road "the most charming and unique of California's gifts to the world."

But soon after World War I the Scenic Railroad began to have a competitor far more dangerous than the distant Alpine funiculars: the private car. The first automobile reached the summit sometime in the early 1920s, bouncing over a rugged wagon track, and soon the good roads followed. Finally, in 1930, the mountain railroad shut down. The last few runs were demolition missions, carrying down the ripped-up ties and rails. Then only the curious curlicued roadbed remained. It is a fire road now. The last of several successors to the original hotel was torn down in the 1950s.

WILLIAM KENT—CONGRESSMAN, progressive Republican, land speculator, and conservationist—became in his time almost the master of Mount Tamalpais. His interest in the peak was warm, incessant, and, it seems, of a double nature. On one hand, he counted on his holdings there to add to his considerable fortune. On the other, he had a tremendous drive to see the peak preserved. Toward that end, over the years, he gave his time and—more important—his land. (In those days, perhaps, it was easier to combine such interests. Kent's land speculations had to do with railroads, and railroads drew tourists, and tourists, after all, need beautiful places to tour.)

At any rate, Kent worked for years on two grand projects. One was to promote and profit from a projected railroad down the far side of the mountain to the town of Bolinas on the Pacific shore. The second was to achieve for the entire mountain the protection of a national park.

At the turn of the century, the Mill Valley and Mount Tamalpais Scenic Railroad had drawn up plans to send an extension down to the ocean. The new road, everybody thought, would make Bolinas the most popular resort in California. Kent, a friend of the railroad directors, began in 1901 to buy up

William Kent's Mountain

33

land along the right of way. By 1904, says Marin historian Jack Mason, you could walk from the family estate at Kentfield east of the mountain to the ocean shore without ever leaving Kent land.

But during these same years Kent was leading a movement to create, at Tamalpais, a national park "on the lines of Yellowstone." You might better say that he *was* the movement. In 1903 he called into existence the Tamalpais National Park Association. Gifford Pinchot, the great forester, was at the founding meeting, along with such San Francisco figures as former Mayor James D. Phelan. Kent's address to that first crowd would have fitted right into the final Golden Gate National Recreation Area campaign, seventy years later. "Need and opportunity here are linked together," he told them. "What would New York or Chicago pay for such an opportunity?"

There was a hitch, of course. The land was private—much of it, indeed, was Kent's—and it would be many years before the thought of buying parkland with federal tax dollars would be thinkable. Some sort of private foundation would have to buy the park and give it to the federal government. Kent wasn't worried. Once the plan was firm, there would remain, he said, "but the slight task of raising money."

Kent continued to speak on these lines for two decades. But not much actually happened except what William Kent, personally, caused to happen.

His interest was tested first at a place then called Sequoia Canyon. This was a moist, sea-facing valley, southwest of the main ridge of the mountain, that was full of redwoods. Though the trees were magnificent—virgin redwoods seem never to be less—they could hardly have attracted much attention in 1840 when Bay Area redwood forests were so broad and so rich that they were an obstacle to travel. But between 1840 and 1870 great waves of deforestation passed over the land. San Francisco was building itself, and much of what went into it was Marin County lumber. The Mill Valley woods went down, and so did the splendid forest around Bolinas Lagoon and most of the valuable timber on Tamalpais itself.

Yet Sequoia Canyon, by luck and isolation, somehow survived into the twentieth century. A high ridge was between it and the bay; it had no easy landing on the sea. The trees remained. By the late 1880s horseback parties were coming to see the grove and the place it created, with its salmon stream, its moss-hung bay trees, its oxalis and azalea, its permanent moist stillness. It had become unique.

In 1903 the property changed hands. The new owner—a friend from the railroad circles—approached William Kent and warned him that the respite was over. The land would soon be sold again. Logging would certainly follow.

Kent was hooked. "The beauty of the place attracted me," he said, "and got on my mind, and I could not forget the situation." He tried to stir up the Tamalpais National Park Association to raise funds for the purchase, but got no help there. So he bought Sequoia Canyon himself, in 1905, for $45,000. His wife, as she herself recalls, questioned the expense. She recorded his answer:

"If we lost all the money we have and saved these trees, it would be worthwhile, wouldn't it?" (He may well have meant it. Later, only half-joking, Kent would urge a governor of California to close the schools for a year and sink the money into redwoods.)

But Sequoia Canyon was not yet, so to speak, out of the woods. In 1907 a local water company sued to condemn the canyon floor—where most of the big trees were—for a reservoir. Desperate, Kent sought help from friends in Washington. Gifford Pinchot, then Secretary of the Interior, proved unsympathetic; so Kent made his case to President Theodore Roosevelt himself, sending him photographs of the endangered land. ("By George! Those are awfully good photographs," Roosevelt responded.) In the end Kent made a present, to the nation, of his Sequoia Canyon; Roosevelt, using a law passed just the year before, declared it a National Monument, inviolable. In a public exchange of letters, the president urged that the monument be named Kent Woods, for the donor; but Kent insisted that it bear instead the name of the famous conservationist, John Muir.

Muir Woods the grove became, and Muir Woods it is now. For millions of people over the years, these redwoods, so close to San Francisco and a stop on every tour, have become *the* redwoods: the only ones they are ever likely to see.

There is an irony in this story. In 1908 William Kent, admirer of Muir, was fighting to keep a dam out of his canyon. In 1914 Kent, by then a congressman, was fighting again—this time to pass the law permitting a dam inside Yosemite National Park, at the place called Hetch Hetchy in the Tuolumne River gorge. In this, the incomparably greater battle, Kent and Muir were on opposite sides. Yet their commitment to conservation was equally genuine. It was not just that the lines of opinion were less hardened in those days (though this was certainly true); it was also that certain painful lessons had yet to be learned. In the ruin that the Hetch Hetchy Project made of the place called "the other Yosemite Valley," we had one such difficult lesson.

Meanwhile, Kent was at work on both his designs for Mount Tamalpais: the railroad land speculation and the creation of a vast national park. Neither got very far. Litigation stalled the railroad for so long that Kent began to lose interest; and though the local press spoke of the park movement as a going thing, it never seemed to bring solid results.

Part of the park plan, however, was carried out by indirect means. Here again Kent was at the center. For years he had been urging that the county create a public water district to replace the unreliable private firms. In 1912, by popular vote, the Marin Municipal Water District was established. (In the same election, Kent was sent to Congress.) In the next few years, the district bought up the drainage of Lagunitas Creek on the east and north of Tamalpais. This rugged forest-bound valley had always been Kent's first priority for park. And indeed, despite the inevitable loss of the natural valley floor to reservoirs,

the water district lands have been used as park ever since. They now amount to some 17,000 acres. Hikers, following several hundred miles of trails, wander back and forth between watershed lands and other public reserves without awareness that a line is crossed at all.

The watershed, however, accounted for only half the mountain. In 1925 a problem arose on the other, coastal side: two minor landowners, neighbors of Kent, announced plans to subdivide. The Tamalpais Conservation Club, a watchdog group begun (with Kent's participation) in 1912, spent four years raising the money to buy the threatened land. The state legislature threw in some acquisition money of its own. In 1930 the property became Mount Tamalpais State Park.

Meanwhile Kent had continued to give land away. In 1920 he gave an addition to Muir Woods National Monument. In 1928 he contributed right-of-way for the road called Panoramic Highway. His last gift, later that year,

was to the nascent state park: 200 acres in the forested canyon called Steep Ravine, north of Muir Woods. It was down this canyon that the Bolinas railroad would have run. The day after executing his gift of Steep Ravine, William Kent died.

Kent's first speculation—on the future of the railroad—had never brought him anything. His second and longer-range hope—for the preservation of the mountain—was to be realized all the way. Conservationists, notably the Tamalpais Conservation Club and later the Sierra Club (its efforts led by Edgar Wayburn), kept the pressure on. After World War II, as adjacent lands were threatened by development, the state park was repeatedly expanded to include them. And in 1973 the National Park Service moved in to buy most of the rest of the coastline from which Tamalpais rises. The park Kent had asked for in 1903 was now complete.

It took seventy years.

THE MAKING OF
THE MOUNTAIN

THE ROCK OF Mount Tamalpais is chaotic: chert and sandstone, shale and greenstone and serpentine, heaped together, it seems, without a scheme. Geologist Salem Rice, who has made a specialty of this mountain, puts it like this: "Any two pebbles you pick up may have started a thousand miles apart and be millions of years different in age."

This is true not only of Tamalpais but also of vast regions of the California Coast Ranges. The jumble, known as the Franciscan Formation, has bothered geologists for years because it is so disorderly. Quite recently they have found an explanation that is satisfactory to most of them.

It has to do with the theory of *plate tectonics*. According to this concept—still quite new—the crust of the earth is made up of about a dozen independent blocks or "plates" that float on semimolten rock below. Some of the plates bear continents, like logs frozen into floes of ice; others are merely fragments of ocean floor. The plates are not fixed. They move, shift, jostle, butt up against each other. Moreover, they grow and diminish.

When two plates collide, several things can happen. Most often one of them buckles, bends, and dives beneath the other, sinking down into zones of heat where it melts and is reabsorbed into the mantle. Where the edge of a plate dives down like this, a deep submarine trench is formed.

Such trenches are found in various parts of the world today. None exists off central California these days, but 150 million years ago we had such a trench. North America—the whole huge immeasurably heavy block of it—was drifting to the west, overtaking and overriding the Pacific ocean floor. It continued to do so for many tens of millions of years.

Meanwhile another thing was happening. Rivers flowed from the continent, eroding successive mountain ranges, carrying sediments into the trench, where they piled up many thousands of feet thick. But the sediments did not lie there undisturbed. They could not. After all, they were in a kind of grinding machine. One side of the trench—the continental wall—was advancing on them; the other side—the descending sea floor—was sinking past them. These motions were fast by geological standards—a number of inches a year—and immensely powerful.

So the sediments, detritus of a continent over long ages, were churned: crammed together, crushed, twisted, subjected to huge pressures, heated, folded. Lava from undersea eruptions added to the mixture, and so did sediments from the sea itself. Fragments of the sea floor were gouged up and added to the pile. Bits of rock that were tougher than the average—and the bits could be several inches or several miles across—kept their solidity and acted like grindstones, pulverizing the rest.

Finally, about thirty million years ago, the motions of the crustal plates went through one of their periodic changes. The result (to simplify a complex matter) was that the relative westward motion of the continent ceased. Later, for reasons that geologists still debate, the offshore trench and its contents were lifted up. The tangled sediments became part of the continent. They make up much of the Coast Ranges of California: the Franciscan Formation.

The Formation has no coherent bedrock mass, only solid chunks or "knockers" in a matrix of sheared or pulverized rock material. If a hill remains much higher than the surrounding land, it is usually because it has inside it one or several solid chunks that resist erosion better than the surrounding matrix.

Mount Tamalpais is one of the hard spots. Its east peak is hardest of all, built of an unusual and very resistant rock called quartz-tourmaline. (Rock climbers love it.) The shape of the mountain is a minor geologic puzzle: its main ridge, with three principal summits, runs almost east and west, cutting across the usual grain of the coastal hills. The experts don't know why.

Mount Tamalpais. From Resources of California *(San Francisco, 1883).*

Point Reyes

O N MAPS, THE big triangular peninsula called Point Reyes seems an appendage, an afterthought, soldered onto a smooth original coastline. Traveling the coast, you may not even realize that it is there. The highway does not follow the sudden outward swing of the shore, but takes a shortcut inland. You could drive this road a hundred times in its green valley and have no notion of what long, wild, bony landscapes, dark with trees or bright with surf and flowers, the ridge to the west conceals.

Between Point Reyes and the rest of Marin County (more or less on the line of State Highway One) runs a vast invisible fissure in the earth called the San Andreas Fault. The San Andreas is no local feature: it is, indeed, one of the few joints in the surface of the planet that are primary. Point Reyes, and thousands of miles of seabed west of it, are part of what geologists call the Pacific Plate: one of the dozen or so huge building blocks that make up the crust of the earth. The Marin "mainland," and all the continent east of it, belong to a second fundamental block, the North American Plate.

The plates are not frozen in place. Slowly, inexorably, the land and seabed west of the fault are shifting to the north. The rate is about two inches a year. But along the faultline itself, friction keeps the immediately adjacent rock masses from slipping smoothly past each other. Even as the vast motion continues, the contact zone stays locked. The edges of the two plates twist and bend, storing the strain like springs. Finally, all at once, the pressure is too much; the rocks leap past each other; the fault slips; and northern California gets another earthquake. The huge 1906 quake, the one that devastated San Francisco, had its center here in Marin. In a few violent seconds Point Reyes jumped northward more than fifteen feet.

In the millions of years that this has been going on, Point Reyes has traveled many hundreds of miles. It is hardly surprising that its geology is different from that of the adjoining Marin mainland: not the jumbled mixture of rock types found on Tamalpais, but solid granite, overlain in large areas with strata of sandstone and shale. The plants that grow on these soils are somewhat different as well: redwoods, common east of the fault, are all but absent from seemingly suitable slopes on Point Reyes. But beyond all this you have the feeling, on Point Reyes, that the whole land is different: separate: a place apart.

On its eastern edge Point Reyes has a fence against the world: thousand-foot Inverness Ridge. Climbing to that long narrow hilltop you rise into a forest of Douglas fir or Bishop pine, the trees not enormously tall but massive, in almost pure stands. This is virgin woodland. Fern and huckleberry crowd the trails. One section of fir-woods is known as the Black Forest, but even this is never dense enough to be dark, and meadows continually break it.

Beyond this shady ridge, you drop down from forest into rugged canyon country, partly wooded, partly brushy with spring-flowering chaparral. Low copses of buckeye and fir are trimmed flat by the wind. There is a curious cluster of natural lakes (backed up by landslides, not by glacial moraines) and also many ponds created to store water for stock.

Toward the west the peninsula narrows. Its middle reach sags as though a weight were on it, and the sea enters the valleys in estuaries, many-branched among the grassy hills. Long fields of lupine and poppies run to the sea. Here is the pastoral part of the seashore, the smooth and gentle part, where cattle still graze. On open slopes you may see the strange white axis deer and the small spotted fallow deer, exotic species introduced by a rancher.

At its far western tip the Point turns rugged again: Point Reyes Headland rises 600 feet above the surf. Point Reyes Lighthouse warns vessels away from this treacherous projection, so far beyond the line of the rest of the coast. The cries of the sea lions, heard faintly from below, sound like a distant human crowd.

North of the lighthouse the Great Beach curves for eleven windy miles. South and east is a gentler shore, broken by the common mouth of Drakes and Limantour Esteros. Here, some historians think, is the spot where the Miwok Indians met and crowned Sir Francis Drake.

The Miwoks, the original natives of the Point, were more numerous here than white settlers ever have been. In the early 1800s the Spanish authorities took them to the missions at San Rafael and San Francisco for Christianization and labor. Few ever returned.

In the 1830s the Point was granted to friends of the new Mexican government. By 1854 one man had gathered enough property together to own the bulk of the peninsula. When he died bankrupt, it was found that the Marin County sheriff had sold his land against debts not once but three times over.

Douglas Fir, Inverness Ridge

43

By the time the matter was settled, the Point was owned in lieu of fees by the victorious lawyer, Oscar Shafter, his brother Jim and his brother-in-law Charles Howard.

For sixty years the Shafters and the Howards were the landlords of Point Reyes (and the leaders of West Marin aristocracy). They divided their domain into ranches (numbered A to Z) and leased them out to dairymen. "Of the outside world," an early reporter recalls, "Point Reyes knew little and cared less, save that it provided a market for butter." That butter, everyone agreed, was the best in California.

The Shafters and the Howards, though, always seem to have been in money trouble. They had little luck with outside investments. Land was their chief asset, but they lived too early to cash in on it. Not that they didn't do their best. They dug for oil and gold. They tried to sell off the timber. They set up sportsmen's clubs and sold memberships. Repeatedly they tried to promote massive development. The Point Reyes Shafter Colony of 1879 — described as "Eden on Earth" — would have carved up some twenty square miles of ocean frontage. A 1905 proposal would have put 10,000 lots on Inverness Ridge (the earthquake helped to burst that particular bubble). But except for small summer colonies on the edges, at Bolinas and Inverness, Point Reyes remained all but unsettled. Maybe the luck of the owners was bad — or maybe the luck of the land was good.

Whatever the cause, the astonishing fact is that Point Reyes reached the second half of the twentieth century almost as wild as it was in the first half of the nineteenth. And as the decades went by, the Point became more and more special simply because it did not change.

In 1935, as the Howard-Shafter estates approached their last disintegration, the National Park Service prepared a survey of possible shoreline parks. The study focused on the eastern seaboard, but the planners singled out Point Reyes for a special examination. Their report was enthusiastic. Fifty-three thousand acres should be purchased, they said, for a federal park, at an estimated cost of $2.4 million. But the idea came twenty years too soon.

The State of California looked at Point Reyes, too, but it was thinking in beach-umbrella terms. Point Reyes, foggy in July, never has been a beach-umbrella place. Nobody, the state concluded, would go there. And so, except for a couple of tiny state and county parks, the land stayed private behind its ranch-road gates.

In 1956 federal interest was renewed. Once more the Park Service was studying possible seashore parks — a list sadly diminished since 1935. The Pacific Coast portion of the survey had scarcely begun when the planners decided, for the second time, to single out Point Reyes. Planning chief George L. Collins put up some of his own money to rush the special report into print. Released in 1958, it called for a major park of some sort on the peninsula. Suddenly Point Reyes was an "issue."

Collins and his crew had reason to hurry. The long quiet, the curious magic that had worked to keep Point Reyes unchanged, was ending at last. West Marin was on the edge, it seemed, of a busy suburban future. The state was talking of freeways to the coast. A subdivision was proposed at Estero de Limantour. Timber had been sold on Inverness Ridge, and the never-logged forests were finally falling. The respite, all at once, was over.

But there was another new factor. By great good fortune, the northcoast counties of California had just elected a new congressman, an extraordinary fellow named Clem Miller. Miller lived in Marin County, knew Point Reyes intimately, and was determined to see it made part of the national park system. He made common cause with Collins and local conservation leaders. And the park's appeal grew.

Could it, though, be created in time? That was the question in the urgent four-year campaign that followed. More than once the chance of failure seemed great. Most established local interests fought the park. On Inverness Ridge the trees kept coming down. The Marin County Board of Supervisors (by repeated votes of three to two) backed the Limantour subdividers and gave them all needed permits almost before they asked.

Not all the park opponents had commercial ambitions. Others were long-time ranchers who asked only to be left alone: to hold on: to survive. "We worked awfully hard," said one ranch wife. "I'm not ashamed to tell you every bit of that land was acquired by the sweat of the brow. If they take my ranches for defense, well, you have to sacrifice. But for recreation?"

This sympathetic argument was weakened by the words of others who were frank about their long-range hopes for the land. One speaker was especially sure of himself. By the year 2000, he told a congressional committee, "there will no longer be a Marin County. There will be a greater city of San Francisco . . . the section we have under discussion today, gentlemen, will be as intensely built over as Palo Alto or Burlingame or San Mateo." It was meant as an upbeat forecast. But it must have acted rather like a threat on the congressmen who heard it.

Meanwhile the forces on the park side kept growing. While Clem Miller pushed the issue in the House of Representatives, Senator Clair Engle advanced it in the Senate. When President John Kennedy took office in 1961, he and his Secretary of the Interior Stewart Udall declared Point Reyes a national priority. In Marin County (with Miller's quiet encouragement) the key anti-park supervisor was recalled by the voters and replaced by a park advocate, Peter Behr, who later became state senator. Again and again Collins and Miller brought official visitors to the peninsula. Again and again they missed the notorious fog and found the weather warm and bright. Gradually the issue became not whether there would be a park, but how large the park would be. A compromise was worked out to allow ranching to continue. Finally, in August 1962, Congress passed the Point Reyes National Seashore bill; Kennedy signed it on September 13. The park was the big model: the same 53,000-acre preserve first called for in 1935.

"It was like the *window* in space shots," recalls Bill Duddleson, a Seashore partisan who was Miller's legislative assistant. "There is a certain limited period of time when the necessary conditions are just right and the shot is possible. Point Reyes had a window: a local congressman who made saving it his first priority, a sympathetic president, a supportive senior senator." He pauses. "Two years later all three men were dead."

Clem Miller died in a plane crash just three weeks after his bill was signed into law. Thirteen months after that, the president was killed in Dallas. Clair Engle died of cancer the following year. The window was closed.

The Perils of the Park

THE NEW PARK was, in two ways, an experiment. And that fact led to two kinds of trouble.

Point Reyes was only the second major unit of the national park system to be created by purchase with federal funds. (Cape Cod National Seashore, authorized just a year earlier, was the first.) Always before, the major parks had been created out of the old public domain or given to the United States by donors. But Point Reyes had to be purchased from sometimes unwilling hands; and in this game the Park Service was a novice.

The $13 million that Congress initially allowed for the job turned out to be far too little. In fact, when the money ran out in 1965, the Service owned less than half the land within the authorized boundaries of the Seashore, and what it had was scattered all over the Point in unusable pieces. Land values, meanwhile, were climbing at fifteen percent a year.

Congress seemed willing to put up more money. But by the time the issue became acute, in 1969, President Nixon had launched an economy drive. The president refused to spend even those park monies he had in hand already. The Park Service became so desperate that it endorsed a budget bureau plan to raise funds for the Seashore by cannibalizing it: $10 million worth of "unessential" Point Reyes parkland, already acquired, would be sold off for development.

Back home the developers weren't waiting. Landowners, justifiably impatient at the long delay, pushed plans forward everywhere at once. On Pierce Point, at the northern tip of the peninsula, 4,500 homesites were proposed. In the south, bulldozers actually got to work at the Lake Ranch. The county authorities declared themselves powerless and looked toward Washington.

But Marin conservationists, headed by Peter Behr, threw together an astonishing ad hoc organization called "Save Our Seashore." By the end of 1969 SOS had presented to President Nixon half a million signatures of Seashore friends and lined up nearly every important voice in California on its side. This time a remarkable number of ranchers were speaking for the park.

Even the California Republican Assembly added its support, and so did Governor Ronald Reagan. Finally, on November 19, the president agreed: the Seashore could be completed.

The delay, of course, had had its price. Property values had been escalating all the while. When the last of the land was finally acquired, the National Seashore had cost not $13 million but $56 million: more than even its bitterest early opponents had predicted. It was a cost overrun worthy of an aircraft carrier. But there is one very important difference: Point Reyes is not, and never will be, obsolete.

It could be a lesson in how *not* to buy a park. (It was, in fact. The same mistakes have not been made again.) But the admirer of Point Reyes, looking back at the wasted years, finds himself not unhappy about the delay. If the park had been completed on schedule, the first Park Service development plans for the land might well have been carried out; and the cost—both in money and in degradation—would have been very high.

Second Class
Park: The Plan
of 1964

POINT REYES AND its eastern counterpart, Cape Cod National Seashore, were experimental in a second way. Not only were they the first two major federal parks to be bought with federal money, but they were also the first two such parks justified specifically (though only in part) as recreational grounds for nearby cities. This raised new issues.

All parks, of course, are recreational areas, and should be. In traditional federal reserves, however, the highest purpose is to keep intact the land and all that lives upon it. Human visitors, while welcome and desired, are to be accommodated only in ways that do not damage the country. This is the ideal: not always fulfilled or fulfillable, it has been at least a constant restraint.

But to promote parks, like Point Reyes National Seashore, that had to be purchased from private owners, their advocates made much of their appeal as playgrounds. These advocates, to be sure, always spoke of preservation as well. The administrators who managed these areas, however, had a tendency to see recreational value only and, indeed, to focus narrowly on the kind of recreation that involves automobile access and crowds.

The new parks were seen by some almost as recreational farms. *Pack the people in. Construct a facility for every conceivable demand. Rebuild the landscape as convenience requires.*

This was the direction the Park Service first pursued as it made plans for its new property on Point Reyes. In fact, the Service classed the Seashore not among the "natural areas" of its system but rather as a special "recreational area"—a technicality that sharply lowered the protective standards.

One thing was wrong. The playground idea simply did not fit Point Reyes. Here was an extraordinary stretch of land and water, a natural treasure that would merit preservation (as the 1957 study noted) "no matter how isolated it might be."

Consider the value of the Point as a wildlife refuge. Two hundred species of land- and seabirds have been counted on the peninsula on a single mid-winter day. Its estuaries, Drakes and Limantour, are healthy coastal wetlands, with the prodigious life that every undamaged wetland yields. Here are beds of the aquatic plant eel grass, food for the handsome marine goose called the black brant. Point Reyes, with the wetlands on it and adjoining it, is one of three small regions along the California coast where eel grass remains in quantity, and where the brant can feed on their annual migration. The rugged coasts, with their sheltered, cliff-backed coves, protect seals and sea lions from human disturbance. Rare spotted owls and mountain lions live in the forested uplands. You could make a long list of threatened or interesting species, concluding, perhaps, with the very local and exclusive Point Reyes jumping mouse.

Set against this the plan of 1964.

Point Reyes was planned as a park for cars, cars, and more cars. The plan had roads for everybody, going everywhere, some new and some rebuilt to higher standards. A four-lane highway would have reached the sea at Estero de Limantour. A clifftop "parkway" would have branched south, traversing the still-wild coast from Limantour to Bolinas (and passing within yards of a major seal rookery). Dune buggies and motorboats were provided for, too.

But the high point of the plan was its "improvement" of Limantour Estero by engineering. One arm of the estuary was to be dredged and blocked with a tidal gate, turning it into a huge freshwater reservoir for swimming and motorboating. The dunes of fragile Limantour Spit were to be "stabilized" with dredging spoil, then covered or surrounded by dressing rooms, concessions, and parking lots. "A Jones-Beach-on-the-Pacific," scoffed journalist Harold Gilliam. In truth that was exactly the idea. Cost of the total vision: an estimated $35 million in 1964 dollars.

Then the money ran out.

THE PARK SERVICE had time, however, to inflict one major scar. This is the bit of misplaced expressway that used to be known as the Road to Nowhere. Today it's the first three-and-a-half miles of the road from park headquarters at Bear Valley west toward Limantour. But for five years after the money drought set in, the road was just a stub of high-priced pavement, ending strangely on the western slopes of Inverness Ridge.

Seen as an urban highway, the Road to Nowhere is nothing to worry about. Hundred-foot cutbanks, tall slopes of fill are nothing new to us. Neither are perennial erosion problems. But here in a major natural park, the construction of such a road (at such expense) was more than a waste; it was a tragedy. It became a symbol of what a "saved" Point Reyes might yet have become—and of what, people swore by the hundreds, it would never be.

By the time the park got its development budget back, the climate of opinion had changed utterly. The public had made it clear that it wanted Point Reyes to be treated as a genuine natural reserve, not as an expendable sacrifice area for busy recreation. Park Service planners, by and large, have fallen in with this idea. Large tracts of the peninsula are classified as formal Wilderness, doubly inviolable under federal law. People on foot or horseback are welcome there. Yet, for all its relative wildness, Point Reyes is getting almost two million visitors a year: about the same number projected for it as Jones-Beach-on-the-Pacific.

Years ago Freeman Tilden, a noted expert on the national parks, wrote some ominous words. "The need for more seashore space for the millions is imperative," he said, "and something has to give, even if conformity is the result."

The Point Reyes experience suggests that conformity need *not* be the result. It suggests that recreation for the many need not mean the degradation of land where natural values are high. And it suggests that people—even by the millions—may neither desire the conformity nor be willing to accept the degradation.

THE SHIPWRECKS

THIS IS NOT a gentle coastline. The landlubber tourist admires it for its ruggedness: its vague immensity in fog, its cold magnificence in wild weather. But, for the captains of a hundred ships, it has been a place of disaster.

The wrecks began in the sixteenth century. Though the U.S. Coast Guard keeps no list, the total of major wrecks by now must far exceed one hundred. Fifty-six large ships have been lost on Point Reyes alone.

If you could raise the vessels, you would see a fantastic fleet: clipper ships, lumber schooners, steamers and modern tankers, even an old Manila galleon. If you could raise their cargoes, you would be rich. Into the surf have spilled silks and spices and French perfumes, porcelains from China and blue-butt redwood lumber from Eureka, gold and coal and dynamite and (more recently) oil. Spilled also, often enough, were their cargoes of human lives. At least a hundred crew members and passengers have died.

Some vessels, anchored offshore, were lifted by storm waves and driven onto the beaches. Some, off-course, simply passed too close to offshore reefs and sea stacks. More than one ship, sails high or engines racing, headed straight into the land with the crew believing, till the impact came, that they were entering the Golden Gate.

First to go down was the *San Augustín* in 1595. When she reached this coast in early November that year, she had already made the passage from Acapulco to Manila and back to upper California. Her captain, Cermeño, had orders to finish the voyage slowly, scouting out safe harbors between Point Reyes and Mexico. Although it was late in the season, his ship battered and laden, his crew near mutiny, Cermeño tried. He anchored off the inlet now called Drakes Estero and reconnoitered.

A few days later a storm came in. Wind from the south carried the *San Augustín* onto the land of Limantour Spit. There she wallowed and pounded and finally went to pieces. Indian middens still yield bits of her cargo, including fragments of elegant Ming dynasty porcelain.

Cermeño loaded the seventy survivors (and the ship's dog) into an auxiliary boat, little more than an oversized dugout canoe, and set out for Mexico. He had no reasonable hope of reaching Acapulco again, in that vessel, in that season; but he did, and without loss of life—except for the dog, which was eaten.

The second wreck came more than two centuries later: in 1841 the *Ayacucho* was lost at almost the same spot. After that, for a century, losses were almost annual. The list is multinational: *Sea Nymph, Norvick, Labouchère, Nahumkeag, Rachel, Erin's Star, Francois Coppée, Selja, Tallac, Samoa, Tai Vin* and *Arakan*. Several local place-names were derived from the names of ships or their captains: Estero de Limantour on Point Reyes, Duxbury Reef at Bolinas, and Tennessee Cove in the Headlands north of the Golden Gate. In 1853 William Tecumseh Sherman, the later general, was shipwrecked twice in twenty-four hours: first in the *Lewis* on Duxbury Reef, then in the lumber schooner he boarded at Bolinas to finish his trip.

The noisiest wreck must have been that of the *Parallel*: when she struck the shore at the Cliff House, her cargo of explosives ignited with a blast heard (it was said) a hundred miles inland. The bloodiest was surely the *City of Rio de Janeiro* in 1901: when she missed the Golden Gate and foundered on Mile Rock offshore from Lands End, one hundred and thirty-one people died. The oddest

Wreck of the Tennessee. *From Frank Soulé,* Annals of San Francisco *(New York, 1855).*

52

casualty was no ship at all but a DC-3 airplane that ditched at Point Reyes Head in 1938 with a loss of five lives.

The government did what it could. The first lighthouse on the Pacific Coast began service on Alcatraz in 1854. Others built were the Point Bonita Light in the Headlands; the Southeast Farallon Light on an island twenty-three miles offshore; the Point Reyes Light; and finally, in 1906, the Mile Rock Light where the *Rio de Janeiro* had gone down. There were sound signals too: cannon at first (fired every thirty minutes when the fog was in); then fog bells; then the modern foghorns with their distinctive noise (like a hugely amplified lowing of cattle). The noise of foghorns seems as natural to the greenbelt now as the fog itself.

The keepers of these lighthouses had little pleasure in their work. At Alcatraz and Point Bonita, the lights of the city, brilliant but unreachable, made the sense of isolation worse. Historian Jack Mason found this notation in the log of Point Reyes Light, January 30, 1889: "The second assistant went crazy and was handed over to the constable at Olema."

The system of lighthouses saved some ships from accident, but the wrecks continued. Only the introduction of radio navigation equipment in the 1930s brought a near-end to them. Even radar did not prevent the collision of two oil tankers under the Golden Gate Bridge in January 1971, dumping 800,000 gallons of oil into bay and ocean. The oil blackened beaches and killed seabirds from Sausalito to Point Reyes.

In the 1960s and the 1970s the big lights, one after another, were automated. The new automatic rigs, usually mounted on the same lighthouse buildings, are small, simple, and self-contained.

Go sometime to Point Reyes Light on its gaunt hogback 300 feet above the surf and the sea lions. The site is famous. So is the three-ton Fresnel lens, which was manufactured in Paris, carried around Cape Horn in a windjammer, and hauled out to the lighthouse in an oxcart. It was the lens, not the light, that turned. Its thousand pieces of glass were cunningly curved to focus the weak radiance of early oil lamps into twenty-four powerful rays. Some of the prisms now are chipped and clouded, and the elaborate brasswork is tarnished from a century of salt air.

A shoreline is too active, too self-cleaning a landscape to give an impression of accumulated history. It is difficult to imagine a beach with ghosts. Not so a lighthouse. It ages; it records impressions of events. Standing in such a tower you think of the vessels that the beacon warned away—and of those others to which no timely warning came.

Point Reyes Light. From Charles Nordhoff, California for Health, Pleasure, and Residence *(New York, 1882).*

Marincello

B Y THE MIDDLE 1960s the outlines of the future Golden Gate greenbelt had begun to be discernible. Point Reyes National Seashore, though incomplete, was a going operation. A little to the south, the state was moving to expand Tamalpais State Park. On the Golden Gate itself, parts of the old Headlands forts were also passing to the state. In San Francisco, veteran conservationist Edgar Wayburn (much involved in all these projects) had already seen the larger possibility: could not these parks be fused together into something more important still?

But even as the wild surmise took shape, it almost failed.

Just north of the first high ridge of the Marin Headlands, between the Golden Gate cliffs and the foothills of Mount Tamalpais, is the place called Rodeo Valley: a rugged hollow in the hills, treeless but rich in flowers, with an almost desert beauty. Its small streams join behind a barrier beach to make a long lagoon, busy with shorebirds and waterfowl. Upvalley, hawks hunt rodents in the tufted grass.

In this valley, in 1966, work actually began on what was to be a city of 18,000 inhabitants. The name of that city was to be Marincello.

Marincello was the vision of a man named Thomas Frouge, a self-made industrialist who had quit school at fourteen to operate a lathe. His construction business, Frouge Corporation, was among the top ten contractors in the nation. Now he wanted to build something grand, and unique, and his own. He was joined in the Marincello enterprise (just to make big bigger) by no less a corporation than Gulf Oil.

Frouge spent the early 1960s assembling the land and readying his plans for it, with the help of a team of planners, lawyers, and publicists. In November 1964, arrangements complete, he announced himself with a massive and highly professional sales campaign.

Glossy drawings and three-dimensional models showed a city unlike anything this largely suburban county had seen. In its original version Marincello would have housed, on the rugged 2,100-acre site, some 30,000 people. There were to be fifty apartment towers and shoals of single-family homes, garden apartments, and townhouses. There would be 250 acres of light industry, a mile-long central mall with pools and elephant trains, and a church-surrounded square called Brotherhood Plaza. Interwoven would be all the schools, shopping, and services that such a population would require. At the summit of the city, on the highest point in the Headlands, would rise a "landmark hotel." Cost of construction in 1964 dollars: an estimated $285 million.

If the first thing that struck you about the project was sheer size, the second was a certain attractiveness. The Marincello plan, by the standards of the mid-1960s, had quite a bit going for it. It was marketed as a "New Town" — a dense, carefully planned, self-sufficient community, in which the ugly mistakes of conventional suburban development would be avoided. Its apartment houses would concentrate people and permit the opening of green expanses. (Nine out of ten acres, the backers claimed, would be open.) "Our goal," said Frouge, "is to make Marincello the most beautiful planned community in the world."

Marincello Model

The "New Town" label linked Marincello to a very appealing theory. Many planners believed then (as many do now) that a growing population should be housed not in suburbs but in new communities well away from the old urban centers: in "New Towns." Each such city would be built from scratch on a carefully chosen site. It would offer housing at all prices; convenient, cosmopolitan shopping; clean industry to strengthen the tax base; plenty of parks; transit systems; up-to-date urban services; and just about anything else its people might require.

Even allowing for the planners' tendency to oversell, the idea is a promising one. But Marincello, despite its label, was not a plausible "New Town." Its economics were shaky. So near San Francisco, it could only have become a commuter suburb, industrial base or no. Its claim to save open space was weak: in saying that ninety percent of the land would be open, Frouge counted as open any ground that was not actually under building foundations. Using a similar standard, many a conventional development would rate as high. What Frouge was doing, in fact, was taking an already massive traditional development and adding to it a ring of apartment towers — sited on land too steep to be otherwise used at all.

However debatable some of its claims, the plan had one undeniable selling point: it would house a large number of people on a fairly small amount of countryside. This, it was argued, would relieve some of the pressure to develop other open land.

In 1964 the people of Marin, alarmed at the steady spread of buildings over their hills and valleys, found this a fetching idea. The argument did not convince everyone; but it convinced enough. Even certain prominent conservationists were won over. The conservative daily newspaper supported Marincello, but so did the liberal-environmentalist weekly: "We expect Tom Frouge to build a city of 20,000 citizens over a twenty-year period which will be a showcase, which will point the way to preservation of the clear and open areas essential and unique in Marin. If he does not, we will be the first to complain."

Just what good the late complaint might have done was not spelled out. Nor did it occur to the editors that this piece of vacant land — the one to be built upon — might be among the more significant pieces of "clear and open areas" not in that county only but in the entire nation. Marincello would not have broken the Golden Gate greenbelt in two — not quite; but it would have destroyed forever that thrilling juxtaposition of urban and wild landscape that is the focus of the mighty park today.

The fact is that nobody — not even the opponents of the project — quite understood what the fight was all about. They tried all arguments, some of them shallow. "We knew we didn't like Marincello," says old campaigner Peter Erickson of Sausalito, "but we didn't know what to offer as a substitute."

And Frouge played the game well. He offered the assumption that the Marincello land could not be, would never be, a part of any park. Everyone, even most of the opposition, accepted it. The question then became: "Do you want a dreary conventional subdivision here, or something bold and exciting?" It was a classic example of how to win by defining the terms of the game.

The victory came with astonishing speed. On November 12, 1965, twelve months to the day after the first Frouge news conference, the Board of Supervisors of Marin County approved the Marincello master plan. Though the county had tinkered a bit, cutting out some of the apartment towers and lowering the overall density, the essence was intact.

After the vote, some conservationists seemed relieved to be rid of an issue that had puzzled and divided them. "Since we are going to have Marincello," one leader said, "we want to see it be as fine a development as possible." But elsewhere a few stubborn workers were joining together to continue to oppose the project. They called themselves the Golden Gate Headlands Committee. As 1965 turned into 1966, they moved on several lines.

- They presented to the supervisors an advisory petition asking the board to reconsider its vote. The 6,000 signatures were ignored.
- In a second petition drive they gathered enough names, they thought, to force a public referendum on the project. But when they submitted this

second petition, the Marin County Clerk ruled some 300 signatures invalid: just enough to stop the referendum. The petitioners went to court, in a long but ultimately unsuccessful suit, to get the signatures reinstated.

• The City of Sausalito, just over the hill from would-be Marincello, filed a second crucial legal challenge. In their swift action on the plan, Sausalito charged, the county authorities had cut some procedural corners. This fact, the town alleged, made the approval void.

Soon both cases were working their way through the courts. But no judge would issue what the opponents desperately needed: an injunction preventing Frouge from setting to work. So men and machines arrived to reshape the hidden valley. A wide access boulevard was laid out. Underground conduits were dug for utility lines. A pair of handsome stucco entry gates were built: gates leading to nothing, but not (it appeared) for long. It began to seem that the outcome of the lawsuits, whatever it might be, would come too late to matter.

THEN — BY SHEER blind luck—there came a break, a change, a pause. Late in 1967 the noise from the Headlands quieted. The work stopped. It was a crucial moment—almost *the* crucial moment—in the history of the greenbelt.

It was not public protest that stopped the work, nor the order of any court, nor even the arrival of fall rains. Thomas Frouge himself brought it to a halt; he could not, after all, carry out certain financial agreements made with Gulf Oil and with another partner. A legal tangle followed that lasted three long years.

We must give thanks for that random quarrel when we look north from Hill 129 and watch the fog climb up the simple clutterless slope that would have been Marincello. For already Marincello's chance was passing. Even as Frouge and Gulf Oil labored on their private issue, the climate of opinion was shifting steadily against their common project. The waverers made up their minds and became opponents. Early backers grew doubtful or changed sides. The greenbelt idea entered the public mind. Slowly, imperceptibly, Marincello began to seem an anachronism, a real but somehow outworn danger, like an old corroded shell that still may have the power to explode.

On January 5, 1969, the remarkable man named Thomas Frouge died in New York. His corporation insisted that its plans for the Headlands were quite unchanged.

In March 1970 the Nature Conservancy approached Gulf Oil, the actual owner of most of the land. Would Gulf consider making the property a gift to conservation? "Taking the initiative now," the Conservancy told Gulf, "is the surest way to disengage Gulf from Frouge." Besides, it would be a tremendous image-builder.

The Turning Point

GATES OF MARINCELLO

FOR TWELVE YEARS they stood in Tennessee Valley at the north edge of the Headlands: the useless but rather handsome gates of Marincello. The entry boulevard would have passed between them, climbing the high bald ridge to the south to reach the Rodeo Valley country on the other side. That road was laid out but never paved. As the scars made by the first construction began to heal, the gates became a curiosity. Hikers, cyclists, sightseers, coming to the trailhead beside them, would look at them, sit in their shade (for even in the Headlands it is sometimes hot) and ask themselves: "Who built these things? What for?"

In time they were showing signs of age and weather. By 1978, as a Park Service planner put it, "it was time to fix them up or take them down." The Service, wisely cautious about destroying structures of possible historic value, called in its experts. The Marincello gates, the experts said, did not have historical significance. Workers came that spring and demolished the two stucco arches.

Most people hardly noticed. A few, remembering the Marincello campaign, felt some resentment and a sharp regret. These odd gates—however modern their date, however unremarkable their architecture—had their own charge of history. They stood for a time that is nearly as remote from us, in terms of public attitudes, as the years when the Golden Gate was lined with guns. It is hard to project yourself back—to understand how such a development as Marincello, in such a location, could have been accepted so easily by so many opinion makers and habitual defenders of open space.

I can remember being much influenced by their opinions. As a youngster I wrote in a high school paper that Marincello was a model for future developments and an experiment that really ought to be made. I accepted as given the idea that this particular land could not ever be put into public ownership. I even agreed that the fog and the wind and the lack of forest made this a poor spot for recreation. In short, I bought the whole line.

The Golden Gate greenbelt is full of historical buildings and places, reminders to us of many important stories. But the story of the greenbelt itself—of the risks it passed, of the way it was almost lost when it was almost won: this is one of the best, and most instructive, of all the stories.

Preserving the gates of Marincello could have helped to tell it.

On November 2, 1970, Gulf and the Frouge Corporation agreed to drop their suits against each other. On the same day, however, a state appellate court ruled on Sausalito's long-running lawsuit against the county. Verdict: the Board of Supervisors had been altogether too hasty in its approval of Marincello. The plan must be submitted all over again. "To invalidate a multimillion-dollar development on a technicality is silly," snapped a counsel for Gulf Oil. But the expected further appeal never came.

On December 22, 1972, Gulf sold its land in the Headlands to the Nature Conservancy. The Conservancy shortly conveyed it to the National Park Service. And the story of Marincello was done.

Destruction of the Gates of Marincello

The Golden Gate National Recreation Area

BEFORE THE LATE 1960s the history of the gradually forming Golden Gate greenbelt is essentially the history of its component parts. Events come slowly and are distinct. People are at work on unconnected conservation projects. Here is one group struggling with Marincello; others concern themselves with the Presidio or Mount Tamalpais or Point Reyes. Hardly anyone seems to see the whole.

About 1969 the separate lines of the story converge. Soon events are following each other so closely that, looking back, you can hardly sort out cause and effect. It is difficult to avoid the feeling that the climax came because it was *ready* to come.

That climax, brought about so swiftly by favorable circumstances and a brilliant campaign, was the creation of the 34,000-acre Golden Gate National Recreation Area: the act that simultaneously completed the vaster greenbelt. Perhaps no other massive conservation project has ever moved so quickly from tentative conception to resounding execution.

The GGNRA project can be traced to three unlikely beginnings: the Nixon administration; the prison island Alcatraz; and a tiny enclave of green land in the city, a vacant military lot called East Fort Miley.

*T*HE FIRST BREAK was the unexpected originality of Walter J. Hickel, President Nixon's first secretary of the interior. When Hickel came to office in January 1969, he was possibly the most controversial appointee ever chosen for a major conservation post. The Sierra Club examined his record as

"Parks to the People"

governor of Alaska, found it hopeless, and led a campaign against his confirmation.

But Hickel began his tenure by surprising people (a habit that would eventually cost him the job). He proved, if not a great secretary of the interior, at least a lively one. From his first days in office he promoted a daring new idea: that national parks should be created not only in wild hinterlands, but on the borders of the major cities. His slogan, and for a time the president's, became: "Parks to the people—where the people are."

There was one problem. President Nixon was minded to spend the minimum on domestic programs, and money for parks was at the bottom of the list. If there were to be "Parks to the People," they would have to come cheap.

This was almost a complete contradiction in terms—and yet not quite. For a few American cities had near them ready-made parks of a sort: military reservations for which the modern need was dubious. One such city was New York, and it was to New York that Secretary Hickel's interest first turned.

Almost immediately, though, his attention was drawn west to San Francisco Bay and the spot of land called Alcatraz.

Alcatraz   OLD MAPS NAME it *Isla de los Alcatraces:* Island of the Pelicans. The Americans slurred the name and made the islet one of the Golden Gate forts. Here they built their first lighthouse on the Pacific, and here they installed the first of the Pacific coastal guns.

But, as the guns got bigger and their ranges longer, Alcatraz became a place behind the lines. More and more it was used for confining people: as a detention camp for misbehaving soldiers or for prisoners of war; as a quarantine base for soldiers with tropical diseases; and finally, for almost thirty years, as a federal prison. Nor was it just any prison. Surrounded by waters thought to be unswimmable, Alcatraz was the lockup of last resort, the place for the men no other walls could hold.

The facility, though, was hideously expensive to maintain, and it was less escape-proof than had been imagined. In 1962 a prisoner (possibly not the first) made it to the mainland. That same year, Attorney General Robert Kennedy ordered the prison closed. "Alcatraz," said the last convict onto the boat, "was never no good to nobody."

President Johnson set up a Commission on the Disposition of Alcatraz Island. It proposed that a monument to the United Nations be built there. But Congress never acted on the plan. Nor did any federal agency (including the National Park Service!) show any interest in taking the island over.

In 1968 the land was offered to lesser governments. The state wasn't interested, but the city of San Francisco was. A tentative deal made, the city government asked the public what it should do with its prospective property.

Alcatraz

Over five hundred suggestions came in—some good, some grim, some funny. Statues were popular: an image of Christ; the UN monument again; a Madonna of the Rock; secular ladies called Justice, Freedom, and Liberty; and a Saint Francis of Assisi a thousand feet tall. Some people wanted "no-nonsense" uses: housing, a bridge anchorage, a garbage dump. Then there were schemes for convention halls, bazaars, cultural centers, schools, and museums. There was even a suggestion to make the island, all over again, a prison.

One large faction wanted Alcatraz to be a natural park. But the mayor and the board of supervisors (anxious to recover the $2 million purchase price) favored commercial use instead. In September 1969 the board fell in with a plan offered by tycoon Lamar Hunt: the island would become a money-making tourist stop, with a "19th-century shopping mall," and an Apollo Plaza celebrating the space program. One critic called the design "a phony space station with a phallic symbol on top."

Alcatraz, old gray hump that it was, turned out to have many defenders. The Hunt plan outraged them. When Alvin Duskin, San Francisco dressmaker and all-purpose activist, placed newspaper ads denouncing the project, 8,000 readers sent in his ready-made protest coupons. The noise of the opposition reached Secretary Hickel. Asked to intervene, he ordered a new federal study.

The short paper, done in November 1969 and titled "A New Look At Alcatraz," began by proposing that the island be a natural park in federal ownership. "We find that Alcatraz provides a unique opportunity," the planners told Hickel, "to further your proposal of Parks to the People."

But they did not stop with this suggestion. "The study of the island," they went on, "has identified another and even more significant opportunity." From Alcatraz their eyes had been drawn to the rest of the old forts around the Golden Gate: to the Headlands, to Fort Mason, and above all to the Presidio. Now they asked for a second study "to determine the feasibility of establishing a Golden Gate National Recreation Area."

There they were: the words: in print. But the report was not made public. Neither was the follow-up study, finished in December, which cataloged the old military lands and their steady occupation by new government buildings. Piecemeal effort, it concluded, could not save the open scenery of the Golden Gate. "A broader, more sweeping concept is needed." And the planners offered, as that more sweeping concept, a Recreation Area of some 4,000 acres, almost entirely land already in federal ownership.

The Indian Occupation

MEANWHILE, ON NOVEMBER 20, 1969, the Alcatraz issue had been forced into a whole new shape. A band of American Indian political activists, claiming to be Sioux, had invaded the empty island and proclaimed it an Indian nation. Their occupation was to last eighteen months.

Of all the strange episodes in the history of this island, this was the strangest. You can read its marks on Alcatraz itself.

A poster from that period still hangs on the wall of the GGNRA headquarters at Fort Mason. It is a photograph of the city across one end of Alcatraz Island (carefully cropped to omit the grimmer evidences of the occupation). There is a tangle of escaped garden flowers, growing with the special luxuriance that comes with fog and the proximity of salt water. Beyond are the bay and metropolitan towers. In the foreground rises a tepee (a form of shelter that the California Indians never used). The legend, glib like the photograph, is nonetheless effective: "They made many promises, but kept only one; they promised to take our land, and they took it."

The Nixon administration responded in a way that some perceived as weak. In fact, it was terribly effective. The administration waited. Within twelve months most of the original occupants had left; the spirit of those that remained had disintegrated; and the island itself was largely a ruin. The occupation had lost all its initial glamour. When, after a year of diminishing suspense, federal marshals took the remnant force to the mainland, there was no bloodshed and (even among liberals) no measurable regret.

But that is not part of this story—the story of the emerging park. It was during the early days, when San Franciscans were still collecting food and clothing for the rebel islanders, that the Golden Gate National Recreation Area became a bargaining point in negotiations between the administration and the Indian invaders.

First of all, the administration offered the Indians a piece of land at Fort Miley. A second proposal came in March 1970. Alcatraz, the negotiators told the Indians, was needed as part of an enormous federal park around the Golden Gate; but the island would be made an Indian memorial, a place to present the Indian historical theme.

The Indians rejected the idea with contempt. A contemporary cartoon shows two San Franciscans watching puffs of smoke drift up from distant Alcatraz. One of them, apparently an old Boy Scout, translates: "It says—you can take your National Park proposal and . . ."

*A*T THIS POINT it was already almost certain that there would be a National Recreation Area. But if the government's initiative had been the only one, the park would have been modest—perhaps no more than an assembly of surplus military lands within sight of the Golden Gate.

Of course, it wouldn't—it couldn't—stop there.

The "Parks to the People" slogan was the first thing that made the GGNRA possible. The second was the interest attracted by the pre-occupation Alcatraz debate. The third necessity, the greatest one, was a popular movement to drive the park concept onward as far as it could go.

This movement might have started anywhere. It might have grown out of the Marincello issue in the Marin Headlands. It might have come directly out of Alcatraz. It might have begun in February 1970 when a roomful of diverse conservationists gathered to protest some new construction proposed by the army on the Presidio. As it happened, the spark was struck two months later in a much more remote spot: at quiet, green East Fort Miley in San Francisco's Richmond District.

Miley is a strip of hilltop just back of the cliffs of Lands End, planted with pine and cypress and hollowed with old gunmounts and buried magazines. Declared surplus in 1948, it went, as did every piece of abandoned military land, to the federal General Services Administration. The GSA sold one piece of the fort to the city and gave another to the Veterans Administration (which built a massive hospital there). The GSA held onto the last twelve acres, called East Fort Miley. Fenced off, signless, this little fragment of green space was not thought of as a park. It was simply there, overgrown and a little mysterious, its value as open space unrecognized.

In March 1970 the agency announced plans to put this bit of "excess land" to some practical use: to build there an archive building about the size of a

Fort Miley and Piffgunnura

67

football field. The plan set off the protest one would hope for in a city crucially short of green landscape. In July, after a not very bitter campaign, the idea was withdrawn.

It was not the first time, nor the tenth, nor the twentieth, that someone had offered to fill the vacuum of military land with some sort of inappropriate development. Nor was it the last time. But the Fort Miley skirmish came at an important moment: it was just at this point that the federal thinking on the Golden Gate National Recreation Area began to be rumored. And so it is this particular issue that dates the beginning of the citizen park campaign.

The campaign had many movers. One was Amy Meyer. Neither a long-time conservationist, nor a hiker, nor a park expert, Meyer was an art teacher who decided, quite in the abstract, to get involved in a community project — any community project. She picked a dilly.

Though East Fort Miley was only blocks from where she lived, Meyer hardly knew the name — not until the archive controversy broke. She first heard of the issue at a meeting of the Outer Richmond Neighborhood Associ-ation, and for the second time at a local Sierra Club meeting where someone asked: "What about the archives?" "There was a silence," Meyer recalls. "I felt sort of obliged to say something." And with that she started what amounted to a new career.

On almost the same day she heard for the first time that the government had plans for a Golden Gate National Recreation Area.

To Meyer and the opponents of the Miley archives, that idea was a strong new hope. It was hope for everyone who had been fighting the perennial and dubious battle to keep open and public the fragments of disused military land from Fort Funston to the Headlands of Marin.

One group active on these issues was the San Francisco Planning and Urban Research Association (SPUR). Meyer turned for help to its executive director, John H. Jacobs, who had what she lacked at that point — experience, personal contacts, knowledge of the political process.

She turned also to Edgar Wayburn, the past president of the Sierra Club, who lived not far from her. While Jacobs had concerned himself with city questions, Wayburn had been working for years on natural conservation issues — among which he ranked the preservation of western Marin. His strategic sense and his knowledge of the working of power, especially in Washington, were awesome.

Soon there was an informal organization backing the Recreation Area and using that powerful concept to oppose the proposals that followed, all that year, for buildings on military lands: not just the archives, but schools, office buildings, apartment houses, and a juvenile detention center.

In January 1971 the group organized itself formally. Meyer was co-chairman, Wayburn the chairman. They chose a clumsy but descriptive name:

People for a Golden Gate National Recreation Area. The unpronounceable acronym was rendered Piffgunnura.

Refining the Plan

MEANWHILE, THE CONCEPT of the Golden Gate National Recreation Area was changing — and growing.

The federal planners were still at work, translating their first vague proposals into lines on maps. At first they proposed a small Golden Gate National Recreation Area under three managements — federal, state, and local. The federal forts, several small state parks, and a number of city parks would be combined under the NRA label, but no property would change hands.

Surprisingly, though, the city proved not only willing but anxious to transfer its coastal parks to the federal government outright. The city, in a budget crisis, could not maintain its lands properly and was glad to give up the burden. So the idea of a solid arc of federal parkland on the San Francisco shoreline was established early.

North of the Golden Gate the federal planners began with the Headlands forts alone. Soon they realized that part of the Marincello property, right next door and very visible from the federal land, would have to be added. Late in 1970 new instructions came from Washington: the park plan should be expanded over Mount Tamalpais to include the state lands there. This plan — it was not public knowledge till another full year had passed — was to become the administration's proposal to Congress.

But Congress, encouraged by People for a Golden Gate National Recreation Area, wasn't waiting.

The Greening of Marin

ED WAYBURN HAD been looking north to Marin for years. Since the early 1960s he had had the goal of seeing the whole ocean coast of Marin County in public ownership. When the Golden Gate National Recreation Area plan arose, he realized quickly that the opportunity had come.

The Marin situation in 1970 was perilous and promising. There were three clumps of public land on that coast: the Headlands forts on the Golden Gate (portions of which had become state parks); Tamalpais State Park, with Muir Woods National Monument and the municipal watershed lands, a few miles north; and, north and west again, Point Reyes National Seashore. A fairly small interval of private ranchland separated the Headlands from Tamalpais; the Nature Conservancy would shortly be acquiring two of the key parcels and was already negotiating for a third, Marincello. Between Mount Tamalpais and Point Reyes, however, there lay a much larger and more ominous gap, still slated, at that time, for urban development.

The two gaps defined two options. It required no great boldness to project a Golden Gate National Recreation Area running from the Gate to Tamalpais, filling the southern gap. But was it thinkable to be more daring?

70

Could you actually reach beyond the state lands on the mountain and fling the new park all the way to the borders of Point Reyes?

To do that, the government would have to acquire ten miles of the pastoral Olema Valley, the soft green country traversed by the San Andreas Fault. Park activist Bob Young of Marin County knew that region well. He had driven it almost daily during the 1969 campaign to complete Point Reyes National Seashore. "I kept thinking," he recalls, "that this valley belonged in the park. But I just didn't see how that could happen. It looked so monumental."

Now it looked like a possible thing.

When People for a Golden Gate National Recreation Area organized itself in January 1971, it had a firm (though as yet unstated) program. The new park would be pushed as far north into Marin County as the public would favor and Congress would finance.

About public favor there was not much doubt. Parks were popular in that first year of the "environmental decade"; Marin County was moving to restrict development on its rural western shore. The way had been prepared by the writings of environmental journalists like Harold Gilliam and Margot Patterson Doss. In early 1971 an article in Marin's *Pacific Sun* mapped the entire greenbelt and urged that all of it be purchased for preservation. The momentum was all one way.

The attitude of Congress, though, had to be probed more carefully. Up to that point, the pioneering GGNRA bills — introduced by Republican William Maillard and Democrat Phillip Burton, both of San Francisco — had included only military lands.

In the late spring Wayburn went to Washington to talk with friendly legislators. With him he took maps of the principal options. It was Burton who asked Wayburn the question he wanted to hear: "Which version do *you* think is right?" Wayburn indicated the most ambitious plan. "Then," snapped Burton, "don't show me the other ones."

On June 29, 1971, Congressman Burton introduced the first bill for the full-scale Golden Gate National Recreation Area including the Olema Valley. Senator Cranston set a similar bill in motion in the Senate. Other congressmen and senators proved avid to add their names to the list of sponsors.

WITH THAT THE decision was virtually made. The lack of opposition was almost uncanny. In 1972 the Nixon administration brought forward its much more modest version of the park, but protested only mildly when this was brushed aside. Even the West Marin landowners testified for the park — aware that their neighbors had made out well financially when Point Reyes was purchased from them. Different indeed from the hurly-burly that surrounded the creation of that earlier reserve!

The Rush to Completion

It did no harm that President Nixon and Republican Congressman Maillard were facing the voters in the autumn. As the election approached, they made their support of the park dramatic.

Only one issue troubled the smooth progress, and that was the Presidio. In their early studies, Park Service planners had argued that essentially all the old reservation could be spared for park use. The army disagreed; and it had supporters. When San Francisco's board of supervisors passed a resolution supporting the park, Mayor Joseph Alioto vetoed it, thinking it too hard on the army.

In the end there was compromise. Most of the fort remained with the army, but any part that would ever be declared excess would be handed to the Park Service without debate.

On October 11, 1972, thus modified, the GGNRA bill passed the House. The Senate approved it on October 12. By October 14, Congress had finished action on the companion bill creating the Gateway National Recreation Area in New York.

On October 28, President Nixon, "with particular pleasure," signed the two bills. Sixty-one million dollars were authorized for GGNRA purchase, $58 million for development.

The official acreage of the GGNRA was 34,000. This figure included all the Presidio, though only a portion actually went to the Park Service. It also included 6,200-acre Mount Tamalpais State Park and 740-acre Angel Island State Park (effective on hoped-for donation by the state). Deducting these lands and others that were parks already, the new National Recreation Area contained some 25,000 acres of previously unprotected land and water.

Few people seemed to realize, even at the final moment, exactly what had been accomplished: that the thing created was not merely a Golden Gate National Recreation Area but a Golden Gate greenbelt of vastly larger scale, fusing parks and open spaces from Fort Mason to Fort Funston and from the Golden Gate to the far beaches of Point Reyes. The greenbelt acreage: about 120,000. It was unique at the moment of its creation. It is unique still.

Adding together every dollar that was ever spent for land in the Golden Gate greenbelt—from the army's first $125,000 for the Headlands through William Kent's $45,000 for Muir Woods to the final $61,000,000 for the GGNRA—you reach a total approaching $130,000,000. Had the greenbelt been purchased at the turn of the century, the whole coastline could have been picked up for a tiny fraction of that sum (albeit in harder dollars). But the nation was then not ready for that. It could scarcely have happened sooner than it did.

Few would doubt that, even at $130 million, our greenbelt was a bargain.

The miracle is that, when the time did come, the grand possibility was still there to be fulfilled.

FOG ON THE GATE

IN SUMMER THE Golden Gate greenbelt has only two kinds of weather. On a given beach or hillside, at a given hour, either the fog is in, or it is not.

When Sir Francis Drake arrived on this coast in 1579 the fog was in. "Neither could we at any time, in whole fourteene days together, find the aire so cleare as to be able to take the height of sunne or starre," complained his chaplain, Francis Fletcher. And it was cool: "We could very well have been contented to have kept about us still our winter clothes."

Many tourists since Drake have been startled at the midsummer chill the mist brings with it, but a two-week overcast is hardly usual. More typically the fog comes and goes each summer day, advancing in late afternoon and burning off in the morning. From day to day its range is altered. Sometimes it barely reaches shore even during the night; on other days it covers the whole Bay Area and flows far inland to the east.

Fletcher, no lover of any weather, hated the fog. To him it was "vile, thicke, and impenetrable." He even claimed, incredibly, that it stank. But if you watch the phenomenon for a few days, you begin to admire it. The fog is a landscape-maker, a display—the best weather-show in this region of equable climate. Its shapes are as dramatic as thunderheads. The fog is always doing something: rising darkly in coastal canyons, spilling over the ridgelines, drowning the Golden Gate, setting the foghorns bellowing, or fraying back toward the sea in the morning sunlight. It has a look of enormous weight. It seems to promise some vast melancholy event, or maybe the biggest storm you ever saw—a storm that never comes.

Under fog the eye picks out other monochromatic things: old grayed buildings, fencelines, windrows of dark trees, grasslands faded in their summer dormancy, and the center of San Francisco with its racks of pale towers. It is like being part of a superb black-and-white photograph. Once you see this coast in fog you remember it (no matter how many sunny days you have also seen) with the fog upon it.

The fog is more than scenery—it is sustenance. In this part of

the West, annual totals of rainfall are small. Summers are long and almost perfectly rainless. If the winter rains were all that watered the vegetation of the greenbelt, large parts of it would be semi-desert—much like California's inland valleys.

But, after the bright warm spring, just at the season of greatest need, the fog brings coolness and, in amazing quantity, water. Researchers say the vapor provides *one-third* of the water supply of these coastal plants—the equivalent, in some places, of ten extra inches of rain. Tall trees, their leaves or needles shedding a drizzle of "fog-drip," do especially well. Without this added water supply, the greenbelt would have neither the redwoods of Muir Woods nor the Black Forest on Inverness Ridge, with its lichen-hung Douglas firs and its undergrowth of fern and huckleberry and salal.

What accounts for this fortunate weather?

The fog is a product of a wind, a current, and a zone of continental heat. On this coast the prevailing wind blows from the northwest, off the sea. In summer, when California's Central Valley grows hot and then hotter, this onshore wind blows more and more strongly: the heated continental air is rising, and marine air is drawn inland to replace it.

The wind from the northwest causes the water beneath it to move in a parallel current, southeast along the coastline. But because the rotation of the earth changes any straight-line motion into a curve—the Coriolis effect—this current veers out to sea as it flows. Between it and the shore, other water wells up from the deep levels below. As every northern California swimmer knows, the water thus brought up is markedly cold.

Across this frigid area the prevailing wind continues to blow. By contact with the cold sea-surface, it is chilled; chilled, it loses some of its ability to hold the water vapor it has picked up from hundreds of miles of ocean. Tiny suspended drops of liquid water form and gather in long masses. This is the fog.

When the wind is weak, the fogbank may be thin, never extending to shore. But when the interior valleys are hot and the wind strong, the fog will be drawn a little farther inland every night until, at last, it reaches the Central Valley and cools the hot plains. Then the wind quiets, the fog burns back to the sea, and the beaches are clear for a while.

The closer you are to salt water in the greenbelt, the more fog you'll see. All the parklands near the Golden Gate—Alcatraz and Angel Islands, the Headlands, the San Francisco shores—are high-fog zones. So is the western tip of Point Reyes, where the foghorn is said to blow one-third of the hours of the year. The Olema Valley and the watershed lands east of Bolinas Ridge are sunnier by far than the fields next to the sea. Because the fog tends to hang low, the top of Mount Tamalpais is sunniest of all.

It is never safe to conclude, because of a clear sky inland, that the beach will also be clear. But a foggy coast has this advantage—it won't be crowded. And once you discover that the fog is, itself, something worth traveling far to see, you will have an enjoyment that too many people deny themselves.

Part 3

The Shaping

What Kind of Park

*T*HE LESSON OF Point Reyes National Seashore—how harsh the penalty can be for late, halfhearted funding—was well learned. The new Golden Gate National Recreation Area got money as required. Land was purchased speedily, mostly from willing sellers. And a rare thing happened. When the last authorized acre was acquired, millions of dollars actually remained unspent.

Rather than lose the funds, park backers went to Congress and asked that the Recreation Area boundaries be expanded to bring in valuable buffer lands. This was done twice in succession. By 1978, the total acreage of the associated parklands stood at over 130,000.

But now that the multiple park was complete, what would be done with it? How would it be put to use? How would the promise—the many promises—be fulfilled?

In 1974 Park Service planners set to work on their new domain. It was clear from the beginning that they could not limit their attention to the newly acquired lands; though parts of it were parks of long standing, and even in other than federal ownership, the greenbelt was an undeniable fresh whole. And the constituents looked different when seen as pieces of the assembled puzzle.

Yet for all that, the new bout of planning was not starting from zero. Its methods, and some of its results, were dictated by an earlier experience: one that this same planning team had gone through, shortly before, at Point Reyes.

*A*S WE HAVE seen, a prior generation of Park Service planners had offered in 1963 a first sketch of the possible future of Point Reyes National Seashore. And we have seen how those almost vandalistic proposals—the dredging and damming of Estero de Limantour, the miles of new highway construction on the bluffs of Double Point—were abandoned, not because of protest, but because of lack of money. In 1970 the money came back, but the early concepts did not. The planning started in again from scratch.

The process that followed was not easy: not for the professionals, not for the public.

Traditionally planners in the parks had had a smooth time of it. They would survey an area, decide what should be done with it and, when given the money, do it. Public hearings came after, not before, the formulation of official ideas. Protest was certainly possible, but it took a lot to make the protest stick.

In the 1970s all this changed, and Point Reyes was one of the theaters in which the change occurred. It is not hard to see why. Never had a national park plan been prepared for a landscape so close to so many interested people. Tens of thousands of people already knew Point Reyes, and loved it, and had definite ideas of what should happen there and what should not.

By 1970 this lively public had had more than a saturation dose of things it didn't like at Point Reyes. The Limantour Estero swimming hole plan was recent enough to be remembered. The infamous Road to Nowhere—the misplaced freeway up Inverness Ridge—was a fresh, eroding scar. Just the year before, Park Service bulldozers had turned a freshwater marsh at Drakes Beach into a parking lot. Even as the planning went on, the incidents continued: not major, but disquieting. There was something insensitive, ham-handed, about the early management of Point Reyes. And the new planning team, not responsible for these annoyances, was a target of the resulting criticism. So was the Park Service as a whole. At one public meeting the regional director was told point-blank: "We don't trust you."

The draft plan published in 1971 did not settle these fears. Not that it was bad; most of the ideas it contained still seemed sound. It certainly omitted the massive engineering schemes of the earlier proposal. Its great drawback was an excessive generality. Depending on the execution, the plan could have yielded a well-made park or a botched one. What people were hungry for— something perhaps never to be had—was surety. The jargon in the document didn't help. It was full of "visitor convergence points" and "vehicular access routes." People asked: "Do you mean roads?"

The writers did, indeed, mean roads; and these became the center of the controversy. The plan, though clean of clifftop parkways, did suggest some additional miles of highway. The major link was a new arterial, called the Muddy Hollow Road, through the center of the park, designed to combine existing dead-end roads into a single system. In addition, the planners wanted to maintain an extensive system of old dirt-surfaced ranch tracks, not for public use, but for Park Service maintenance vehicles.

The opposition, led by the Sierra Club, wanted no new highway, and far fewer miles of service roads. And it wanted most of the Point Reyes Peninsula placed, by Congress, in the highly protected special status called "Wilderness": a zone that forbids most development and motorized access.

When the master plan was formally adopted in 1972, the opposition had won few points. But the debate did not stop there. It moved on to Congress. At last in 1976 the lawmakers created an extensive Point Reyes Wilderness and, in the process, killed the Muddy Hollow Road. Well before that final decision, it was clear that there would be no road, and that most of the peninsula would grow, if anything, more wild.

What was being decided, in those years, was the function of Point Reyes in the larger greenbelt that, even as the controversy continued, was growing up to surround and absorb this older park. The Seashore, it was clear at last, was not to be a multiple-use park with something for everybody; rather, it would be the back country, the remotest room of the many-chambered recreational mansion.

Something else was decided at Point Reyes. The rocky course of that debate made it clear that the following round of planning—the round that concerned the whole completed greenbelt—could not merely be carried out

Beach Grass, Limantour

by professionals and then offered to the public for approval or protest. "There's no way we could have gotten a plan through," says greenbelt planner Doug Nadeau, "without involving everyone."

NADEAU HAD REASON to know. He had been head of the Point Reyes planning team; in 1974 he became co-leader of the greenbelt planning group. He and his colleagues had learned. To Nadeau, the public was now the client, "and I would never design a garden for a client," he says, "without talking to him first."

In most national parks it is hard to define the "client." People travel for thousands of miles to visit the Grand Canyon or Yellowstone; they are not the permanent neighbors of the parks they visit. But in the Bay Area most of the users of the greenbelt are also its neighbors. As the Point Reyes controversy showed, this does not only make it possible to treat the public as client; it makes it essential.

Congress recognized this need. When it established the GGNRA, it provided also for a Citizens' Advisory Commission. Its members represent the users and defenders of *all* the greenbelt parks, including Point Reyes. Though this commission was not given formal authority over the planners' work, the team did, in fact, report to the citizens' group and follow its direction.

Further, the planners set out to draw the interest of people who would not ordinarily have been park-watchers—but for whom, in rhetoric at least, the park had been created. Chief among them were inner city people and their organizations—Blacks, Chinese, Japanese, Chicanos. "They wouldn't have bothered us," Nadeau recalls. But the Park Service, aided by outside consultant firms, went to great lengths to reach these people and call their attention to the choice being made.

First step was to build a file of thousands of groups—homeowners' associations, neighborhood organizations, recreation clubs, interest groups of every variety. Choosing a cross section of these, the planners sought invitations to speak at meetings. These were not public hearings, managed by the professionals; instead the Park Service people came as guests. They did not present ideas but asked for them. It worked. "We got more response and information at those small meetings," Nadeau remembers, "than we did at any other stage." The year 1975 was spent making these contacts, while consultants did backup planning work of various kinds.

The second phase came in 1976. Fifteen workshops, lavishly advertised, were held. Here the Park Service ran the show. After some orientation, people were asked to take a stab at park planning: not merely to say what they wanted or expected, as they had done before, but to show what needs should be accommodated and where. The planners thought this would be the most valuable part of the whole operation—the payload. It wasn't. Instead, they found—as planners seem often to find—that people prefer simply to make the case for what they care about, and not get into the harder business of juggling zones and uses. There seems to be a natural limit here to planning-by-the-people: a point at which the professionals must take over.

N OW THE PLANNERS boiled down the hundreds of separate suggestions they had gotten from the public, together with some of their own. The result was a set of possible alternative plans, usually four, for each distinct sub-area of the greenbelt. These they would present to the public once more, before drawing their own conclusions.

Alternatives

Door, Fort Point

This trick of defining options, and getting reaction to them before venturing further, is a commonplace of planning these days. The method can be good and bad. Clumsily defined, such alternatives can confuse the real choices rather than make them clear. But the Golden Gate staff did an excellent common-sense job: the alternatives actually did reflect the four dominant points of view.

One natural viewpoint was that of the *Preservers of Land:* people who watched anxiously over all pristine and near-pristine landscapes. These, they argued, must be maintained or, where already damaged, restored.

A second group was the *Historians.* Preservers of another sort, they were concerned most of all with the historic scenes and buildings in the greenbelt: these must be protected, repaired, explained. (This is an awesome charge. Planners found that they had in the Golden Gate greenbelt a historical resource second only to that in the parks and monuments of Washington, D.C.)

Hang-glider, Marin
Headlands

And there were the *Recreationists*. These people pointed to the promise of "Parks to the People." To fulfill it, they wanted access, facilities, things to do, places to play. Some were inner-city dwellers who were cruelly short of recreational space. Others were recreational vehicle owners, tennis players, dirt bikers, fishermen, dog walkers, hang-glider pilots: just about anyone with a favorite thing to do and a shortage of land on which to do it.

The fourth informal party might be called the *Friends of the Status Quo*. These were people who were already using the park in some fashion and liked it fine just as it stood: old people who were at home in a crowded but familiar social center in Aquatic Park in San Francisco, long-time hikers on Mount Tamalpais, users of semiprivate stables in the Marin Headlands.

This division into parties is artificial and oversimple. Though these were indeed the dominant concerns, it is plain that almost everybody belonged to more than one persuasion. No one insisted that all the decisions should go one way. When the alternatives were presented to the public, people were invited to mix and match, and they did. The question was one of proportion, of balance.

In June 1977 the Citizens' Advisory Commission held hearings on the alternative plans. The planners did not, they say, learn much from them: the same ideas were repeated. The staff knew now (as well as anybody could) what the client wanted. Now came the actual planning job—the laying-out, to continue Nadeau's metaphor, of the client's garden.

Two years later the planning team published its Draft General Management plan. As we go to press, a last round of public hearings is to be held. Though some unresolved issues remain, no one expects the acrimony, the tension, that marked the comparable hearings seven years earlier concerning Point Reyes.

What we saw in the case of the Golden Gate greenbelt was a test of a new kind of planning. It had to be called a success. People's ideas were listened to; they knew it; and they responded warmly. As for the planners, they seemed convinced that they themselves profited: that the results are better because of the years of meetings: that the process was not (as well it might have been) a mere diversion, a political exercise meant to prevent controversy.

It must be admitted that the Golden Gate greenbelt was an easier subject for such an experiment than most other parks would have been. There was a remarkable public consensus about what should happen in the new park complex. (Maybe the most difficult issues had been fought out already at Point Reyes.) And the park itself, with its diversity and generous size, made planning easy. Few questions, it seemed, took the form of a cruel "either-or."

*T*HE NEW PLAN starts with what is most obvious about the multiple park: that it is a range, a progression, a spectrum. It can be divided into three parts. At the south, on the coasts of San Francisco, are lands that are intimately part of that city. These get, or at least should get, heavy public use, and cannot, even in metaphor, be called wild. Across the water, in Marin County, Angel Island and the Headlands make a borderland. Though much less altered from nature than the city lands, they are also bound to be used heavily. Without

The Bones of the Plan

prohibitive expense, they can be made easy for city dwellers to reach. From the point of view of an inner-city neighborhood, it is exactly this border zone that justifies the money spent on the greenbelt.

Beyond the Headlands the vast third region of the park extends: Mount Tamalpais, with its swarms of hikers; the watershed lands behind the mountain to the east; to its west, the pastoral Olema Valley; and west again the great elbow of Point Reyes, the wilderness climax.

Each of the three zones has particular requirements. The San Francisco lands, though spectacular by setting, were mostly in rather poor shape when the Park Service acquired them. The old city parks were run-down and under-staffed; the military lands were cluttered and sometimes dreary. Lucky accidents and long campaigns had maintained the coastal rim in public ownership, but little was being done to maintain it in good condition. On the San Francisco perimeter the need is clearly to restore, clean up, open up, repair.

At the wilder end of the park the requirements are different. Except for the correction of damage done by old abuses like overgrazing, most of this land needs only to be left alone. The need is not to solve old problems but to prevent new ones from occurring as millions of visitors discover the country that is newly theirs.

Between the city and the wilderness is the accessible middle zone, the point of contact. Much of this land is fragile enough to need some protection; yet it is here that the public demand for easy access is most valid. This is the region of the park where the balance will be hardest to find, the risk of failure most troubling.

Such problems are made easier because of the park's great artificial resource — its hundreds of old buildings. The planners have found that fully a third of the buildings are historic and worth saving. Thus there is almost no need to build anything new in the park. Whatever the price of past development in environmental degradation, it has already been paid. There is no way to go but up. As the park is "developed," many buildings will actually be removed. There will be more open land, not less.

But one very important thing is lacking to make the park the public resource it is intended to be. That is mass transit: buses certainly, possibly ferries, possibly trains. The park has all the roads it is going to have (new ones would never be permitted by the Bay Area public, even if the Park Service wanted them). There are already incessant traffic jams. And people who don't own cars — especially the city people whose needs the park is largely intended to serve — are cut off from their own greenbelt.

On this point everyone agrees: a transit system is as essential to the Golden Gate park complex as is the land itself. But progress in creating such a system has been slow. Of all the problems of the park, this is the most intractable.

*T*HE DEVELOPMENT PLAN for the Golden Gate greenbelt is, in many ways, a modest scheme. Nothing large and dramatic is likely to be built; not many portions of the park are to be boldly transformed. The plan, then, is not something you can sketch in broad black lines. It exists in detail.

To visualize what the planners have in mind, imagine a tour of this most varied landscape: showing what it is and what it is to become.

Golden Gate in Fog, Presidio beyond

RETURN OF THE BEASTS

Gathering Murre Eggs. From Charles Nordhoff, California for Health, Pleasure & Residence *(New York, 1882).*

TWENTY-FIVE MILES off the Golden Gate lie the scattered granite islets called the Farallones. On a bright winter day they seem to jut up a few yards offshore, precise and black; in hazy summer weather you may not see them at all.

The Farallones (from the Spanish for cliff or headland) are today a National Wildlife Refuge. For seals and sea lions, for seabirds in the tens of tens of thousands, they are a sanctuary unequalled for hundreds of miles.

The islands were not always so protected. In the early 1800s, Boston Yankee sealing parties descended on the chain. They took uncounted skins of the sea otter and at least 150,000 pelts of the fur seal. Later the Russians, based at Fort Ross, moved in, harvesting not only skins but also meat from the sea lions, oil from the carcasses of the huge comical elephant seals, and down from seabirds of many species. At the end of the Russian period, as far as we can tell, the original seven species of mammals on the Farallones had been reduced to three. The northern fur seal, the Guadalupe fur seal (though some doubt it was there to begin with), the sea otter, and the elephant seal were all locally extinct. Only the harbor seal and the California and Steller's sea lions remained.

Pressure then shifted from the mammals to the birds. Beginning in 1848 the highly palatable eggs of the common murre were harvested by the shipload. By the end of the century, when the traffic was outlawed, fourteen million eggs had been removed and the murre population was crashing.

In the twentieth century a slow recovery began. It was kept slow, in part, by a continued human presence. On Southeast Farallon, the largest and most significant island, were a lighthouse and a colony of several Coast Guard families, with cats, dogs, and feral rabbits—not much of a wildlife sanctuary. Oil pollution, too, was killing birds as early as 1911.

Things got better in 1972, when the Farallon Light was automated. Today, instead of the Coast Guard staff, a tiny research team from the institution called the Point Reyes Bird Observatory is stationed there to keep off poachers and "recreational" seal-shooters and to study the shifting populations of birds and mammals.

In 1972, also, a major piece of good news emerged: the northern elephant seal, which had not bred on the islands for 150 years, had once more begun to raise young there. Northern fur seals have also recently reappeared; if they follow the pattern of the elephant seal, they may someday stay to breed. The birds have also continued to recover. Once again the Farallones, crowded with cormorants, auklets, guillemots, murres, make up the largest seabird rookery in the United States outside Alaska.

With the Farallones as an example, it is natural to wonder whether some of these species—especially the big marine mammals—will reestablish themselves on the mainland of the Golden Gate greenbelt as well.

They were there once. Steller's sea lions are known to have bred on Seal Rocks; elephant seals had colonies north to Point Reyes; sea otters were common. Today the harbor seal is the one species that breeds on, or near, the greenbelt's mainland.

Since records kept in the past were poor, it is hard to discover a trend. But cautious observers see promising signs. Several species are almost certainly increasing and spreading. Scientists are watching for the first breeding of the elephant seal along this shore. The sea otter, once thought to be extinct, is working its way slowly north from Big Sur. There is reason to hope that this coast will someday be richer: that these strange mammals of the sea will give the greenbelt another distinction.

This hope is countered by a paradoxical worry. Compared with the alternative of urban development, the parks along this coast are indeed wildlife refuges. They keep the habitat open for reoccupation. Yet the presence of human visitors sometimes drives the animals away again. The snowy plover, for example, nests on open beaches and tolerates no interference. Harbor seals abandon the shore at the slightest disturbance. The young of the seals and sea lions are vulnerable: the alarmed adults can trample them in their rush to escape intrusions from the land.

It is not an easy problem. The public needs to understand it and needs to judge fairly the competing values of access and protection. We can afford to moderate, in certain places, our desire to see the land, to touch, to physically enjoy. If we have to zone ourselves out of some remote cove or estuarine shore in order to preserve fragile wildlife, we should be willing—even proud—to do so.

Sea Lions. From Charles Nordhoff, California for Health, Pleasure & Residence *(New York, 1882).*

Survey and Outlook: The San Francisco Side

*I*T'S ABOUT TWELVE miles around the San Francisco shoreline from the lawns and quiet water of Aquatic Park to the dunes and breakers of Fort Funston. It seems much longer. The scene changes quickly on that coast, and often: from garden to forest, from beach to headland, from architecture to open space. Each of the separate properties that are now combined in the coastal greenbelt has its own history, its own sharp character.

It is easy to get to this arc of shore, at most points, by transit; and if Park Service transit designs are carried out, convenient shuttles will actually run along it. But for a closer survey of what is, and of what is to be, imagine a long traverse on foot—a day-long walk from Aquatic Park to the Golden Gate and on south to Funston, where the sandstone cliffs rise over the muscular ocean.

Aquatic Park

*F*OR A CENTURY this eastern anchor of the coastal strip was known as Yerba Buena Anchorage. It was on this shore in 1775 that Captain Juan Manuel de Ayala made the first Spanish landing on the future site of San Francisco. After the 1906 earthquake and fire, the original cove was filled in with the rubble of Chinatown. Then in the 1930s much of this grim fill was removed to create a new rounded embayment. The spot was developed for recreation by Franklin D. Roosevelt's Works Progress Administration.

Aquatic Park today is a simple place: a long curving pier for fishermen and sightseers; a sheltered cove for occasional swimming; a lawn and garden; a strip of beach. Here also is the San Francisco Maritime Museum, a white-painted building vaguely shiplike, and, on the Hyde Street Pier, a flotilla of historic ships: the sail-powered lumber schooner *Alma,* the likewise wind-driven bay scow *Thayer,* and several more—working vessels that hauled lumber or passengers or salmon under steam and sail. Nearby nautical shops sell compasses, anchors, caulking irons, fids, and hawsing beetles.

The Park Service plans major though gradual changes at Aquatic Park. It will remove a number of minor buildings and a good deal of pavement. The present Maritime Museum, a cramped and inconvenient building for displays, will become a recreational building, with rental fishing gear and other equipment for water sports. The museum collections will move to the huge and handsome Haslett Warehouse, a historic building on the inland edge of the park. Haslett, in fact, will become the chief visitor center in the greenbelt. This spot, the planners reason, is the park's front door. When you step off the Hyde Street cable car, you will enter the greenbelt's world.

Window, Fort Mason

NEXT DOOR TO the west is the wooded bluff of old Fort Mason. Mason, fortified first to defend the neighboring anchorage, has been a military post since Spanish days. Along with some dull military buildings due for destruction are others that are gracious and historic. In one of them Senator David Broderick died in 1859 after the strange and famous duel with Judge David Terry. In another old building is the headquarters of the Golden Gate National Recreation Area.

Until 1973 a chain-link fence blocked the pathway from Aquatic Park to the army's Fort Mason enclave. Now the fence is gone and the broad paved walkway is part of what is called the Golden Gate Promenade — the three-mile pedestrian route along the water from the Maritime Museum to Fort Point at the Golden Gate.

You begin the path by climbing along the bluff under rows of hundred-year-old cypresses. Below is a touching oddity — about six hundred feet of the original rocky bayshore, never altered or filled. This is the one spot, the only spot, where San Francisco's natural coast on San Francisco Bay remains as it was. Everywhere else the sand-colored rocks, the pools and the seaweed have given way to a new and regular shoreline built of fill. The uplands of Fort Mason, now rather crowded with buildings, will be opened up considerably under the new management. The fort will be a greener contrast with the crowded urban slopes just inland. Lawns, gardens, windbreaks, benches, picnic spots will spread. The remaining fine old buildings will have various uses: exhibits, a hostel, a seniors' center, and space for community organizations to use as they will.

AT THE WESTERN foot of the Mason bluff is the next bit of shoreline: artificial, ugly, useful, and (in its own way) historic. From these three massive piers, one-and-a-half million soldiers shipped out in World War II alone. The spot, with its parking lots and pinkish-painted warehouses, is not elegant, but it turns out to be one of the great resources of the greenbelt. Sheltered indoor space for public use is hard to find, and here there is 300,000 square feet of it. The planners rejected proposals to tear out one or more of the piers and the associated buildings. Instead these will be cleaned up, painted, and landscaped.

Who gets the use of all that precious space? There was a lively competition for it. The Fort Mason Foundation, representing various cultural groups, argued for arts-related programs and events. Environmental spokesmen favored uses having to do with the sea: research programs, exhibits and shows, headquarters space for organizations concerned about marine ecology. Other people, including neighborhood groups, asked for indoor play space, especially courts for informal team sports.

The Park Service found itself in a good position in the debate: it could afford to satisfy almost everyone. Since there were three main uses pro-

posed—recreation, culture, ecological study—why not give one of the three piers to each!

The area already houses public and semipublic groups such as community theaters, art galleries, and conservation organizations worried about whales. In summer the Park Service encourages special events such as circuses, concerts, fairs.

Marina Green

WALKING WEST FROM the piers on the Golden Gate Promenade you come next to the San Francisco Marina and its Green: a long rectangle of lawn beside water busy with sails. This is one of the most popular and populous parks in the city. Much of the waterfront here is taken up by yacht slips, and at one point the "park" is only a sidewalk wide between a city street and the pleasantly creaking boats. Yet the link remains.

The Marina is still run by city authorities, and most people seem to like it that way. Should the city ever transfer it to the Park Service, the federal planners have only a few changes in mind. One would be a major improvement: they would rearrange the areas of grass and pavement so that the green could run right to the edge of the bay, rather than being cut off (as it is today) by roadway.

Presidio Coast: Crissy Field

WEST OF THE Marina the waterfront walk continues on the long bare shoreline of Crissy Field. Part (not enough) of this old army airfield, fringed with little-known and charming beaches, has been granted to the park. The swells in the bay are a little larger here; the Headlands of Marin—high, dark and wild-looking—begin to dominate; and always you look toward the grand red silhouette of the Golden Gate Bridge. It is good to be here at evening, when the water turns gray, the offshore buoys flash on, and a last few boats tack in toward harbor. From inland, just at sunset, come the sounds of a bugle and the discharge of a single gun.

In spite of the grandeur it looks toward, Crissy Field is a part of the park that plainly needs work. The land is old bay fill, in itself featureless. Army buildings crowd against its inland side. To make the best of this magnificent site, the Park Service needs at least a few more acres of the bordering military land.

The planners had to choose between two appealing options at Crissy Field. One was to make the area as natural and wild, at least in appearance, as it could become. The second approach was to make a landscaped urban park out of the field: a Marina Green without the boats and cars. The public was divided. In the end, the plan to civilize was chosen. There will be lawns, windbreaks (very important here by the Golden Gate), artificial hills, clumps of trees, places to sit and places to eat, and probably a shallow lagoon for safe warm-water wading.

AS YOU WALK on west, the filled strip narrows; the modern shoreline converges on the green embankment that marks the original edge of the land. You run out of level ground at Fort Point, the northern horn of the San Francisco Peninsula. Here, in the shadow of the bridge, is the fort itself. This handsomest of the Golden Gate fortifications, three stories of red brick and whitish granite, has a little of the look of a Romanesque church. It strongly resembles another fort, Sumter, which was taken by the South at the start of the Civil War. Indeed, Southern sympathizers in San Francisco made an attempt, clumsy and easily thwarted, to capture Fort Point as well. It would have been a prize. From these blank portholes ninety guns were set against the Gate; another thirty-seven showed their muzzles over the rooftop parapet.

When the time came to build the Golden Gate Bridge, the fort was obsolete; worse, it was in the way. The army was willing to have it torn down. But bridge designer Joseph P. Strauss loved the old squat tower for its fine stonework. To save it, he built a special and otherwise unnecessary arch into the understructure of the bridge. Now at Fort Point you look up at Strauss's arch, humming with the traffic on the deck above.

Fort Point

Fort Point is the boundary of bay and ocean. On certain tides the big combers turn the corner of the land and shatter on granite breakwaters inside the harbor mouth, drenching an occasional parked car. Just east, in the lee of the fort, is the Fort Point Coast Guard Station. From it, fast cutters set out to rescue boats and people in trouble (it happens amazingly often) both inside and outside the Golden Gate.

Along with a museum and tours, Fort Point offers an intriguing special program. Student groups stay overnight to experience briefly the rigorous life of the old garrison. These "environmental living" classes, enormously popular, are booked many months in advance. Similar programs—designed to show how history was lived by soldiers, settlers, Indians, ranchers—will be available at numerous places in the greenbelt.

Presidio Coast: The Ocean Side

AROUND THE CORNER from Fort Point the landscape is immediately rugged. Cliffs, covered with bright green coastal scrub, drop to small curved beaches. The northern coves, nearest the bridge, can only be reached by scrambling or bushwhacking. Baker Beach, a mile to the south, is broad, accessible and heavily used. But the whole region of shore seems most un-citylike. It is continually startling to look back and see the great busy structure of the bridge: it seems out of place, like something added to a photograph by double exposure.

The proposed park plan will try to keep this tang of isolation. But it will also make this lovely coast more usable. Paths will be built for cyclists, joggers, and pedestrians. Obstacles—rubble, fences, some uninteresting small buildings—will be removed. The gray emplacements on the clifftops will remain. At Baker Beach, Battery Chamberlain will be restored, complete with a 95,000-pound gun that rises and sinks on its "disappearing" carriage—the only such gun you'll find in the greenbelt today. Inside the same battery (in curious juxtaposition) will be a sheltered space for group events.

The Presidio Interior

CRISSY FIELD, FORT Point, and Baker Beach were all once parts of the big military reservation known as the Presidio, which fills the northern angle of the city. Park advocates wanted much more of the Presidio to be transferred to the National Park Service. In a last-minute congressional compromise, only the coastal strip was in fact transferred; but the entire Presidio was included within the nominal boundaries of the Golden Gate National Recreation Area. Any inland area the army relinquishes will go to the park, not to any other use.

Even today, the Presidio functions as part of the larger greenbelt. Much of its splendid open landscape is available to the public. Its forests, planted a century ago on barren dunes, show green against the white-stacked buildings of the city beyond.

96

AT THE SOUTH end of Baker Beach you leave the old Presidio and lose, all at once, the pleasant sense of remoteness. Ahead lies the Seacliff residential district. This handsome neighborhood, itself a San Francisco attraction, was in one respect ill-planned: it occupies the coastal bluffs completely and severs the hitherto continuous strip of parkland. One public enclave within this development — James D. Phelan Beach — is an official part of the GGNRA. To reach Phelan Beach or continue the coastal walk, the pedestrian must follow city streets.

Lands End

After this interruption the greenbelt resumes with the varied district of Lands End and Point Lobos. Here the coast swings briefly into an east-west line; you look northeast across a bight of ocean to the Golden Gate, due north for miles along the windblown spray-hazed coastline of Marin. It is one of the city's remarkable views.

The shore here is a band of forest and precipitous rock, backed inland by a wide city-owned golf course. The undergrowth in spots is almost jungly — the plants partly native, partly escapees from gardens. The only intact middens of San Francisco's Costanoan Indians are found near here; so are gun emplacements of the turn-of-the-century period, on Fort Miley, the former military reservation. Inland, on the edge of the golf course, is the Palace of the Legion of Honor, a famous art museum.

Once there was a railroad along these cliffs. Later a road was laid out, called El Camino del Mar. The railroad is gone, and the highway, laid out on an unstable hillside, has buckled and slid away. Both arterials are now pedestrian routes, quiet walkways through the woods. This is a spot from which the city has retreated.

At Lands End as at Baker Beach, the Park Service plans a general cleanup but no essential changes. It will cart away rubble, take down the fences that mark old property lines, add paths and seats and shelters from the wind. The old roadbed of El Camino del Mar will be a bicycle path; the railroad bed, a hiking trail. At Fort Miley, an old half-buried magazine (a cavernous structure where ammunition was stored) will be turned into a stable. There will be a jogging trail, picnic tables, and at the old emplacements the usual explanatory exhibits. It might be worth adding one more exhibit: one identifying East Fort Miley as the spot where the Golden Gate National Recreation Area campaign properly began.

Sutro Country   AT THE SOUTH end of the old road and railroad is the curious district created by San Francisco's nineteenth-century Mayor Adolph Sutro, eccentric, populist, philanthropist, silver king. Here, behind a pair of heraldic lions, is his hilltop estate, now a public garden and ocean overlook. Nearby is Point Lobos (not to be confused with the Lobos near Monterey). Sutro built here also, carving the headland with stairs for walkers and with channels to carry the water thrown up by the violent Lobos surf. He made a display of the sea, a kind of wet fireworks.

Between Sutro Heights and Point Lobos are the foundations of the famous Sutro Baths, a swimming palace in the old mayor's time, later a skating rink, and now a ruin — the complex burned to the ground in 1966.

The last and dominant object in this crowded corner of the city is the Cliff House. The building you see now is not Sutro's. His, long since lost to fire, was Gothic, half-timbered, seven stories tall. The present Cliff House is less than an echo, squat and blocky. But you find yourself charmed by the odd combination of grace and cheapness, honkey-tonk and genuine attraction, that fills the place.

Six hundred feet offshore are the Seal Rocks, another world. Wherever you go in the Sutro region you hear the barking of the seals and sea lions that crowd these surf-washed sea stacks, unconcerned with the busy shore. Without Sutro's protest, the seals would all have been shot in 1889 for eating commercially valuable fish.

HERE THERE WAS real controversy. A slight majority of the public favored a lavish multimillion-dollar job of restoration: the Cliff House to again become an imposing Gothic tower; the Baths to rise up again from their ruins. A group called Citizens for Sutro Landmarks got a thousand signatures on petitions calling for such restoration. The idea even had the backing of Friends of the Earth.

The Park Service workers were intrigued; but they decided, in the end, against these plans. The huge cost was part of the problem (though it might have been undertaken with private money). The other objection was that congestion would increase hugely in a newbuilt Sutro district. When the original structures were built, access was by train. But today the region already has more auto traffic than it can handle: there is a perpetual fuming snarl around the Cliff House.

The planners instead favor a handsome modern building on the Cliff House site. This would be the only sizable piece of new construction in the entire park. For Sutro Baths they propose a landscaping job: a park on the ruins, using foundations, pools, fountains and waterfalls. Across the road, the Sutro Heights park would remain much as it is.

Maybe the least satisfactory thing about the Sutro region today is the major road that runs through it, cutting the Heights off from the Cliff House. It would seem a good long-range idea to shift that thoroughfare to the inland side of Sutro Heights. As it is, the image that is likely to stay with you, after a visit to this corner of the greenbelt, is of a traffic jam.

Plans for Sutro Country

SOUTH OF SUTRO'S bluff the land subsides and rows of houses parallel the shore. For the next three miles the greenbelt is a strip of beach and dunes a few yards wide, between the surf and the road called the Great Highway. It is here that many visitors from eastern states get their first look at the Pacific Ocean. Golden Gate Park, San Francisco's magnificent urban garden, adjoins the beach for a few blocks; so does the city zoo.

Ocean Beach is one of those parts of the greenbelt that should be more beautiful and more hospitable than they are. Here, in fact, the Park Service faces some of its most difficult management problems.

Ocean Beach

Once, a broad area inland from the beach was covered with active dunes. In summer, wind blew loose particles from the shore and added them to the nearer ridges of sand; in winter, powerful waves would undermine the dunes and take sand back. In this seasonal exchange, the dunes nourished the broad beach and were nourished by it.

When San Francisco expanded to the sea, the builders did their best to override this natural system. They leveled the inland dunes for housing and pushed excess sand into the water, shifting the shoreline a few yards to the west. More important they laid down, very close to the waves, that broad swath of pavement known as the Great Highway.

The natural system continues to operate, but now it operates, by the standards of our convenience, in a destructive way. In the summer, as always before, sand scours off the beach and blows inland; but now it settles on the highway and must incessantly be bulldozed off. Only four of the original eight lanes are ever kept open, and often the road is shut down completely. In the winter the vigorous waves, as always before, undermine the sandy shore— but now they are also undermining the Great Highway itself.

Both problems are increasing. Some experts feel that the shore is merely changing back toward a lost equilibrium; others point out that the sea level is slowly, minutely rising. But whatever the ultimate cause, it is plain that the beach is shrinking. Visibly. Inexorably. Piles of concrete blocks and other fill, placed in an effort to slow the erosion, succeed mainly in making the shoreline ugly.

There seem to be two possible answers. One is to invest many millions of dollars in an elaborate system of seawalls or "artificial headlands" (defending the coast, not against enemy ships, but against the ocean itself!). The second possibility is to decide—against all cultural habit—that the coastal processes must be given room to work: to allow the restoration of the missing nearshore dunes; to remove our structures from the zone in which the seasonal sand exchange takes place.

How much land would have to be cleared? Because the erosion picture is not completely understood, nobody knows for sure. The specialists believe, however, that there is a line of equilibrium, and that it lies not too far inshore. It would almost certainly be necessary, however, to reroute—or to abandon —the Great Highway.

Here enters a complication. The jurisdiction of the National Park Service ends at the highway's western curb. San Francisco has sole control over the road itself. And the city has major plans for that corridor.

San Francisco has a pressing sewage treatment problem. When its original drainage system was installed, rainwater runoff was channeled into the same pipes as the actual sewage. In the wet season the treatment plants can't handle the tremendous overload, and raw sewage spills out through many outfalls. Many of these, incidentally, are on the coast of the Golden Gate National Recreation Area.

The problem desperately needs to be solved. The preferred solution is to build a tremendous underground storage vault into which the excess winter flows can be diverted until the treatment plants catch up with the backlog.

Now the catch: the city wants to install this vault—a great rectangular tube three miles long—in the sand under the Great Highway. But this puts the structure in the zone of coastal erosion; and erosion experts are coming to the conclusion that the vault would be exposed to the waves in a very few years. In this case the Park Service itself—as owner of the adjacent beach—could be held responsible! To the Service planners it seems clear that the sewer structure must not be built along Ocean Beach. In late 1978 the issue was far from resolved.

Aside from the erosion problem, the future of this coastal strip is a major issue. The Great Highway, intended to be a gracious recreational boulevard, is instead an eyesore and an obstacle to recreation. San Francisco's own planners would like to scale it down to four lanes and relieve its dreary straightness with some curves. The federal team (which has no jurisdiction) feels that only two lanes should be retained, and these used only for buses.

Whatever the outcome of these debates, certain minimal improvements will be made. More pedestrian crossings will be added. Toilets and other simple facilities will be installed. An attempt will be made to stabilize the remaining dunes—to the extent possible without a resolution of the basic erosion problem.

AT THE SOUTHERN tip of Ocean Beach—and of the entire Golden Gate greenbelt—the coastlands rise again in cliffs. The rock of them—if it can be called rock—is a fossil-rich sandstone so soft that you can write in it with a finger. Wind and sea are swiftly cutting back this malleable stone. On the highland above are dunes, partly covered with sea fig, beach grass, and some of the city's most interesting wild flowers. A tunnel runs through one tall dune: the emplacement of Battery Davis. Nearby are the missile silos of a later decade, also obsolete.

Fort Funston

Funston, popular with walkers, is the one spot in San Francisco that shows the original dune landscape, neither leveled off nor landscaped to an artificial green. It is popular with hang-glider pilots, and with the sightseers that come to watch them, because of the powerful updrafts along its steep escarpment. The flyers, lying flat in their harnesses, can circle for many minutes over the breakers below.

The fort does not give the planners many problems. The chief concern is to avoid adding artificially to the steady but acceptable natural erosion. Planners propose merely to lay out formal paths (keeping walkers off the fragile vegetation) and to build a wooden platform for the crowds that come to watch the glider pilots leaping under their brightly colored fragile wings.

101

ADOLPH SUTRO AND THE OUTSIDE LANDS

THE HISTORY OF nineteenth century San Francisco seems to center on a few bold characters, a few great names: rascals, financiers, philanthropists, winners and losers of huge fortunes, mighty fools.

One of those figures, less rascally than most, was Adolph Heinrich Joseph Sutro, whose properties at Lands End now belong to the Golden Gate National Recreation Area.

Sutro, a Jew from the Prussian Rhineland, had many talents. In Germany he had built a textile plant and had shown real promise at the piano, drawing the attention of the composer Mendelssohn. After the European revolutions of 1848 he became a refugee, and in 1850 he arrived in San Francisco.

In 1859 the Comstock Lode was discovered in northern Nevada. Unlike California's easily panned gold, the silver of the Comstock required elaborate processing. Sutro, then a tobacconist, helped develop a good treatment: the Randohr-Sutro Process. In 1861 he moved to Nevada and bought a mill.

There he found a larger challenge. The exploitation of the lode was hampered by a huge underground reservoir of scalding water. To drain this reservoir, Sutro proposed to dig a four-mile tunnel, 2,000 feet below the surface of Sun Mountain.

He took the wild scheme to the great monopolist William Ralston, head of the Bank of California. At first Ralston supported the project. Then, sensing that Sutro might challenge the bank's control of the Comstock, Ralston set out to thwart him. Astonishingly, Sutro persevered. Doggedly, slowly, he found backing; doggedly, slowly, he got his tunnel built. Completed in 1878, it did everything he had claimed. The victory, though, coming even as the Comstock petered out, was almost too late. Turning bearish at exactly the right moment, Sutro sold his tunnel stock early enough to get the still-substantial price of $700,000.

Back in San Francisco, the miner turned to real estate. Soon he owned almost a tenth of the land in the city. But his special interest was in the unsettled western region: the "outside" lands.

Exploring that coastline with his daughter Emma, he came

upon a windy bluff with an endless view. Just below it was a hotel, much declined from its previous elegance, known as the Cliff House. Sutro bought them both. San Franciscans thought it a preposterous investment: "Sutro's Folly."

On the high bluff he expanded an existing country house and laid out an elaborate garden. He planted palms from New Zealand, pines from the Mediterranean, and eucalyptus from Australia (even importing a shipload of Australian soil). His taste in statues was just as exotic. He set them up by the dozens: satyrs and nymphs, Dianas and Cupids, fairy-tale heroines and characters from Dickens. Some of these were copies of great masters, some the purest Victorian *kitsch*. In 1885 he opened this odd park—this place of costly and unselective culture—to the admiring public.

His second project was the Cliff House. Accidents forced a more total restoration than he had had in mind. In January 1887 the schooner *Parallel,* carrying some forty tons of explosives, blew up on the rocks below the Cliff House porches and knocked down one wing of the hotel. On Christmas Day 1894, a fire destroyed the remainder.

In 1896 Sutro completed the spectacular replacement, an elegant seven-story chateau in French Gothic style. It was elaborate, even florid; but in the old photographs, silhouetted against clouds and the gray simple sea, it looks handsome indeed.

Sutro Heights and the Cliff House were two points in Sutro's triangle; the third was Sutro Baths next door. Its huge indoor basins, where sea water was warmed by sunlight under the glass roof, were unlike anything the still-rough West had seen. "The baths rival in magnitude, utility, and beauty the famous abluvian resorts of Titus, Caracella, or Diocletian," wrote one admirer. "Thus has the tide been harnessed and made subservient to the multitudes."

The multitudes got to this complex by streetcar. The fare, for years, was a nickel. But in 1893 the private streetcar line was sold to a subsidiary of the Southern Pacific Railroad, and the price quadrupled to twenty cents. To Sutro, as to many San Franciscans, this bit of larceny stood for everything he hated in the railroad: its dominance of state and city politics, its immunity from legal challenge or restraint, its utter disregard of public or consumer interest. Sutro fought. He fenced his property and charged twenty-five cents admission to anyone who came on the SP line. By this pressure tactic he drove the fare down to a dime. Next he got a franchise to build a line of his own.

Sutro's quarrel with Southern Pacific made him a hero of sorts. In 1895, drafted by the New Populist party, he ran for mayor and won. Then his troubles started. He was used to giving orders;

seeing things done; fighting definable enemies. As mayor, with limited powers, he could not function. He left office in 1897, not seeking a second term. Two years later, Adolph Heinrich Joseph Sutro died.

Gradually his little empire went to pieces. The Cliff House rode out the earthquake of 1906 (with $300 in damage) but burned down in 1907. Its modern successor, a sort of blockhouse, has none of the outrageous charm of the old Gothic. Up on the grounds of Sutro Heights, the gardens fell into disrepair. ("Let's go out to Sutro's," they used to say, "and steal statues.") The house was razed in 1939. The Baths lasted longer: they were operated until the mid-1950s, and burned down in 1966.

What remains is the still-gracious hilltop park, the quickly aging ruins of the Baths, the walking trail on the railroad bed, and the tunnels and sluices that still capture the surf at Point Lobos (though the water no longer funnels into the Baths). We have also a portion of his library, once containing some 250,000 volumes.

Dr. Emma Sutro Merritt, the mayor's daughter, purchased Sutro Heights from other heirs and deeded it to San Francisco, effective 1937. The National Park Service received this as a gift from the city in 1973, and later purchased the Cliff House and the Baths.

Up on the Heights, four statues remain: a stag, a Diana, and the two oddly gentle lions that face each other across the entry gate.

Survey and Outlook: The Islands

*T*AKE A FERRY to an island—Alcatraz or Angel.

Angel Island is a smoothly sloping knob of land covered, mostly, with hardwoods: live oak, buckeye, bay, madrone, and red-berried toyon. (The army imported eucalyptus, pine, cypress, and a few palm trees.) From a coast of coves and tiny beaches, the island rises to a peak a little higher than the towers of the Golden Gate Bridge, three miles away. From the summit you see cities in every direction.

Sir Francis Drake—according to one group of Drake scholars—may have walked on Angel Island in 1579. Two centuries later, in 1775, Captain Juan Manuel de Ayala was here, but did no walking: having unwisely shot himself in the foot, he stayed on board at a cove now named for him while his crew explored the far reaches of San Francisco Bay.

Angel Island early became government property. During the time of the big guns, army headquarters was at Camp Reynolds on the Golden Gate side; the island had three batteries. Meanwhile, on the opposite shore of the island, immigrant Chinese built a shrimping camp. To add to their income, they probably smuggled whiskey to the garrison. At Point Blunt on the island's southeast corner was a whorehouse.

In 1898 the army established East Garrison; it was chiefly a transshipment port and sent thousands of troops to the Pacific as late as the 1930s. Also on the east shore was an immigration station, the "Ellis Island of the West." Most recently the island had a Nike site.

Finally federal authorities ran out of uses for Angel Island. By 1962 it had passed to the State of California for use as a park. Angel Island State Park, like

Point Reyes National Seashore, had its planning controversies. In 1970 the state proposed a scheme of massive development, including a restaurant on the 780-foot summit. This brought the predictable sharp protest, and these ideas were dropped. But it was partly the alarm at these early state concepts that caused the island to be included within the nominal boundaries of the Golden Gate National Recreation Area.

Thus, though the land remains with the state and is likely to continue to remain so, both state and federal planning teams have been studying the island.

This time neither group wants to change things much. A monumental Statue to Peace—proposed for this site as well as others—will certainly not be built. Ayala Cove, the spot where all ferries now discharge their passengers, is getting too much trampling; in the future people will also arrive at East Garrison. The buses that now circle the island on the long loop road may be replaced by horse-drawn vehicles. Campsites will be provided (for the first time), and slips for the overnight mooring of boats, and perhaps a hostel. The use of the island will grow considerably, whoever controls it.

Some of the hundred-odd buildings on the island (most of them over a century old) will be preserved; others will be razed. The area of pavement on the summit (disconcerting after the pleasant hike to the top) will be removed. An attempt will be made to eradicate the spreading French broom and eucalyptus.

If there is any contrast between the emerging state plan and the concepts advanced by the federal Park Service, it is that the Service planners would prefer to have a little less of everything: fewer camping spots and mooring slips, fewer facilities, not quite so many people on the island at one time. And the federal team would like to completely abandon the overused landing at Ayala Cove, making this corner of the island relatively remote. But the state-federal differences are by no means major.

Alcatraz   NO PIECE OF land in the multiple park drew as much attention as twenty-two-acre Alcatraz Island. "There are people," the planners noted, "who believe that, whatever is finally done with Alcatraz, it must be highly symbolic of something." But there was no agreement what the symbol should be, or say.

The planners rejected, once and for all, the proposals for grandiose monuments. They also rejected another romantic plan: to clean the island to its rock and give it back to the birds. Instead, they proposed to retain not only the nineteenth-century fortifications and the old lighthouse—what you might call presentable artifacts—but also the main cellhouse of the prison days. This is the building that one angry member of the public described as "a memorial permanently enshrining all that is degenerate."

It is interesting to note how federal attitudes have changed. The early report on Alcatraz done in 1969 concluded: "Shorn of the unsightly evidence of its unpleasant prison past, and redeveloped with winding walkways and vista points, it can become a perfect spot from which to enjoy the beauty that surrounds it." Now the planners see the whole past of Alcatraz—even its darkest and angriest years—as a story that ought to be told.

The right decision, I think, was made here. I was able to see the island very nearly at its grimmest: not long after the unhappy fading-out of the Indian occupation, when it seemed to be nothing but ruin piled on ruin—charred buildings, piles of junk, wall-slogans, rubble. It impressed me greatly. I found myself wishing that something could be done to petrify the island at that moment in its history: the low point, the nadir.

It is a curious fact that as events cross the border that separates *news* from *history* we begin to see them not as agonizing issues but as fixed things, almost as objects. And the places in which they were enacted seem to change. An Alcatraz, gray as it is, becomes a kind of statement, like a canvas by Goya, a play by Brecht, a Picasso *Guernica*.

The impulse to sanitize the past—to clean it up, to prettify, to remove the traces of indignity or tragedy—is natural enough. But so is the impulse that tells us to value history for what it is. These events are ours. These things happened to us: proceeded from us: are part of us.

And so is Alcatraz.

Survey and Outlook: The Marin Side

*T*HE GOLDEN GATE Bridge is a showpiece, a monument. You almost forget that it is also, and first of all, a road. It feeds Highway 101, the massive commuter artery of the North Bay, into and through the Headlands of Marin. The highway runs east of the main ridge of the Headlands, halfway between the ridge and the water of the bay. It does not enter the western and larger part of the rugged region.

*F*ROM 101, JUST as you reach the Marin shore, inside the Golden Gate you look down east to Horsehoe Cove, and a cluster of red-roofed buildings called East Fort Baker. At this writing still an army post, Baker will someday be the point at which most visitors reach the Headlands: the main door to the parks in Marin as Aquatic Park is the door to the greenbelt in San Francisco. Shuttle buses will converge on this cove, and ferries will travel to it from Fort Mason and other points across the water.

   This will be a spot to get information, food, and rental gear (including bicycles) for fun or further traveling. A private marina will become public: more slips and a boat-launch. As usual in the park there will be more demolition than building, and the finest structures will be saved. There may eventually be a campus for retreats and conferences, similar to Asilomar near Monterey.

East Fort Baker

FROM *FORT BAKER* two narrow roads take you under the freeway and west into the larger ocean-facing region of the Headlands. The first, Conzelman Road, climbs right across the face of the Golden Gate itself; this is the way to the tunnels and overlooks of Hill 129. You will seldom see so many people taking pictures as you will along this road. Photographers even come at night to set up their tripods—in the darkness, the city shines and the bridge lays a shadow across the lights reflected in the water. At one point a gated sideroad drops to a beach neither on the bay nor on the ocean but precisely at the Golden Gate—Kirby Cove. The spot has had guns in every generation of harbor defenses.

The second road west from East Fort Baker climbs no hills. Instead it goes under them—straight through the thousand-foot central ridge in a narrow, echoing tunnel a mile long. The army excavated it to haul the long guns of Battery Townsley to their site on the sea. Inland you emerge suddenly, blinking, into the hollow center of the Headlands: Rodeo Valley. The road follows the valley's small creek past military buildings, a rifle range, and a pair of lagoons (one fresh, one salt) to end behind a wide brown beach. To the south is guano-white Bird Island, the city invisible around its point. To the north are the hills that Marincello would have covered. Trails climb into them.

In order to reach this point today, you must drive. But the Park Service is determined to make this place easy to reach by bus, and even, in times of heavy use, to keep cars away. Otherwise this will not be a park, but a parking lot.

Rodeo Valley, in the new park plan, has a particular function, one that no other spot in the greenbelt precisely serves. Neither urban nor wild, it is to be a border post, a place of introduction. Here inner-city visitors, some of them actually afraid (psychologists tell us) of large open spaces, will be shown the edge of wildness.

In order to serve this purpose the valley cannot, itself, be wild. It must be easy to get to, easy to use, comfortable. It will have the same sorts of conveniences found on the San Francisco side: food and places to eat it, shelters from the wind, some limited indoor lodging, even trails designed for the blind and people in wheelchairs.

The need for access has led the planners to discard one thought listed among the early alternatives: the closure of a mile of road, making Rodeo Beach an easy walk-in. A similar logic caused them to approve stocking the two lagoons with fish (fishing is especially popular with urban visitors). Boardwalks will be built to spare the streambank vegetation from trampling.

Making this borderland available to people (the Park Serivce feels) is not enough. People must actually be brought here, be shown how to do things, have things pointed out to them. There must be "outreach programs." The historic buildings that will remain after the thinning of the present clutter will have a variety of consonant uses: overnight summer camps, a group retreat, artists-in-residence, an environmental center. The YMCA and the Yosemite Institute are already here. So is the Marine Mammal Rescue Center, a hospital for seals and sea lions. Special events—folk festivals, symphony concerts—will continue to be held at several outdoor sites.

There will be a couple of walk-in campgrounds—the sort where you carry your gear a few hundred feet from bus or car—and at least one hikers' camp, up on the ridgelands.

NORTH OF THE square mass of the Headlands, the Marin hills fall off to a valley so low that there was talk, during World War II, of digging a canal through it. (The area is named for the freighter *Tennessee,* wrecked on this shore in 1853.) *Tennessee Valley*

The public road into this valley stops halfway to the coast, leaving a pleasant couple of miles to walk, past an operating ranch and another small lagoon, to a tiny cliffbound cove. The valley floor was the northern edge of the Marincello property, and it was here, at the end of the road, that the gates of that never-never city were built. From the roadhead, joggers and cyclists and walkers head in all directions. Steeper trails rise south into the Headlands and north toward Mount Tamalpais.

Plans for this area are modest. The Park Service hopes to remove the ranch buildings eventually. There will be a hike-in camp for the long-distance backpackers, and a small model farm in the branch canyon called Oakwood Valley. A private stable near the roadhead is controversial but may be allowed to remain.

NORTH OF TENNESSEE Valley a new ridge begins. Curving north, it marks the divide between the built-up bay shore of Marin and the quiet coastal drainages. Then, suddenly, Mount Tamalpais bulks ahead, thrown up like a roadblock across the prevailing grain of the coastal ranges. *Tamalpais*

From the south and west sides of the mountain flows Redwood Creek, a sizable stream with a good run of silver salmon; it passes through the red-woods of Muir Woods and reaches the sea at the tiny community of Muir Beach. This is the first of several coastal villages that perch, somewhat uncomfortably, on the expanse of public green. North of the creekmouth the west end of the mountain slopes 2,000 feet to the sea.

Mount Tamalpais has several owners. The inland, eastern/northern slope belongs entirely to the Marin Municipal Water District, and there is no thought of seeking its formal addition to the shoreline park. The coastal side is managed partly by the state and partly by the National Park Service. Tamal-

Grassland, Mount
Tamalpais

pais State Park, within the formal boundaries of the Golden Gate National Recreation Area, may or may not become federal; but (as at Angel Island) the federal planners have considered it anyway.

Since most of the Tamalpais region has been park or quasi-park for years, the mountain has a large clientele. People seem to know what they want. "Everything on Tamalpais," one speaker said at a hearing, "has been developed by people's use over many years — which is far better than planning, if you have the time."

Actually, if you could lay out Tamalpais all over again you might want to thin out the system of mountain roads. Highway One, the Coast Highway, reaches the shore at Muir Beach and follows it on to the north. Panoramic Highway, an alternate route, stays high on the mountain's western shoulder. Ridgecrest Boulevard continues north on Bolinas Ridge and joins the cross-county Fairfax-Bolinas Road. There are roads to the summit and down Redwood Creek, past Muir Woods. This is a lot of pavement for what is, after all, a small mountain.

But, accepting the general layout as fixed, the Park Service considered only fairly minor issues in deciding what it would do with the region if it were consolidated in federal hands.

One issue drew most of the attention: camping. Almost everybody wanted more spots to stay overnight. Accordingly, the planners offered several new sites, either walk-in or hike-in. (Because of an erosion problem, the traditional site at Pan Toll would be closed.)

Curiously, the best campsites are found not on the park side of the mountain—the south and west—but on the north and east, the municipal watershed side. Camping used to be allowed there on several natural grassy flats. But in the 1960s, troubled by fire danger, an invasion of squatters, and pollution problems, the water district closed its lands to any overnight stays.

WEDGED INTO THE angle between Mount Tamalpais and the southern end of the Point Reyes peninsula is little Bolinas Lagoon. This is one of those pieces of terrain in the greenbelt that has been fought over incessantly. In the 1960s local citizens and regional conservation groups turned aside a plan to transform the quiet square-mile wetland into an urban harbor, with rows of slips, restaurants, motels, turning-basins, and (fitted into otherwise useless corners) "wildlife refuges." More modest plans for harbor improvement have also been controversial. Some say that the lagoon is filling in so rapidly with sediments that it needs a little dredging to survive at all; others are skeptical.

Bolinas Lagoon

The body of Bolinas Lagoon, marsh and mudflat and channel, now belongs to Marin County. The county plans to leave it alone. On the east shore is Audubon Canyon Ranch, a private preserve set up to protect a rookery for herons and egrets. As you pass by on the coast highway, you see the big loose birds spread out like white cloths in the canyon's redwood trees.

Two villages, Stinson Beach and Bolinas, occupy most of the land around the lagoon that isn't in park. People who live here used to worry about saving the surrounding land. Now they worry about saving the character and savor of their towns. For these people the arrival of the parks did not settle all controversies, but, on the contrary, set up new ones.

How can a village inside a park—its main street perhaps a park road— hold on to a special nature, a sense of self? It's a problem wherever large parks and small towns come together. In most places, the faction that welcomes change and sees profit in the traffic—a faction always present—sets the policy. This has not been so in Marin, least of all in Bolinas.

The majority in Bolinas has a simple desire to be left alone. Since the early 1970s the town has been run by a combination of environmentalists and rather self-conscious members of the counterculture. The story (told by Orville Schell in the readable history *The Town That Fought to Save Itself*) is by turn engaging and exasperating. There's a little of everything in the Bolinas mix— common sense and nonsense, genuine feelings and shallow mystical mouthings, justified grievance and impossible isolationism.

When the Golden Gate National Recreation Area was created, many in West Marin were skeptical. When the Recreation Area was expanded, the skeptics became outright opponents. They fought the last round of expansion as they might have fought an oil refinery. "The federal government is the enemy," wrote a local columnist.

When the voices become this strident, you tend to stop listening. But there is a middle way. The small towns of western Marin can never be as they were before the parks were created; but where park policy can lessen the pressure on them, this should be done. In the case of Bolinas, the Park Service will not pretend that the parklands near the town (including the southern part of Point Reyes National Seashore) do not exist. But it is willing to leave this part of the greenbelt a backwater, and to make the access road that skirts the village a distinctly secondary route.

The Bolinas controversy is not a unique case. It hints at a problem that will come up many times again, and that must be considered whenever a new park is planned in a landscape already occupied, already cultural, already used.

Bolinas Lagoon

The Olema Valley　NORTH OF BOLINAS Lagoon extends the green Olema Valley: darkly forested on the west, where the barrier hills of Point Reyes rise; more open eastward. The Coast Highway runs the length of it, rolling up and down low humps. The valley has no spectacle; it does have interest and charm. Millennia of motions along the San Andreas Fault—the Point Reyes side advancing to the north—have given it a puzzling topography. Two streams drain the trough, one flowing north, one south; but motion along the fault has carried their headwaters past each other. Now they flow parallel, yards from each other, in opposite directions. Here too is the historic town of Olema.

At the north end of the ten-mile lowland the highway reaches the town of Point Reyes Station and the end of the greenbelt. Nearby, at the old Bear Valley Ranch, is the headquarters of Point Reyes National Seashore. The northern end of the valley is actually easier to reach than the center—a better road comes across the hills from eastern Marin.

Nobody wants this region to change much. It will remain pastoral. Planners hope that ranching will continue under leaseback. They would like to arrange public tours of a working ranch; failing that, a facsimile ranch could be set up, a "demonstration farm." Bear Valley will remain a center, with an information building, self-guided trails, a reconstructed Miwok Indian village, and the farm where Morgan horses are bred for use throughout the national parks. At the south end of the valley, near Bolinas Lagoon, the historic buildings of Rancho Bolinas will probably become an environmental education center. Hostels will be placed in a couple of old ranch houses. The plan also calls for walk-in campgrounds near the road, with permanent tents at one of them—a convenience for minimally equipped campers. For hikers there will be a camp somewhere on Bolinas Ridge to the east.

THIS IS NOT the first plan for Point Reyes. It is the third, really an update. The old controversies have defined the nature of the place: few roads, a good deal of ranchland, a lot of wilderness. Though half the acreage of the combined greenbelt is on Point Reyes, it attracted only a tiny portion of the comment. The attitude was "Don't mess up a good thing."

In the future, as today, there will be only four important roads into Point Reyes: one to Point Reyes Light on the far western tip, one to McClures Beach near the northern headland, one straight west from Bear Valley headquarters to the beach at Limantour, and one past Bolinas to the southern roadheads at Palomarin. According to plans there will soon be fewer cars on those roads, and more buses. Transit, as usual, is seen as the saving possibility. Any hint of a facility that would draw more cars, or provide more room to park, has been unpopular.

This northern end of the greenbelt will not have the generous services provided in the southern parts such as food service, boat moorings, equipment rentals. (There is already one hostel.) Even simple signs interpreting history or natural features were criticized by the public. As somebody said at a hearing: "We don't *want* to be told everything."

As at Mount Tamalpais, camping was a serious issue. There are now four camps—Sky, Coast, Wildcat, Glen—and one hostel. Camping is allowed only within the grounds and in specified slots. The camps are pleasant but not very private. Minor roads, open to service vehicles, penetrate to them. If you go to them expecting a strong flavor of wilderness, you may be disappointed.

With so many people looking for places to camp, there could be no

Point Reyes

possibility at Point Reyes of actually satisfying demand. But the experience could be made more satisfying to the wilderness-minded.

Many people urged that the peninsula be opened, here and there, to the kind of unstructured camping you would undertake in more distant wildlands like the Great Smokies or the Trinity Alps. The planners were tempted. But in the end they turned down, at least for the moment, the primitive camping experiment. This kind of use in so heavily used a park would, they reasoned, require extra rangers—and extra money.

They do plan, however, to open four new camps of the type already present, accessible only by trail (or in one case by canoe). You will still check into a given slot, as at a motel, but the slots will be a bit more widely scattered.

In 1978 a long awaited moment arrived. The tule elk, the original grazing beasts of the peninsula, were reintroduced to a range on its northern tip. In the old days the elk had numbered in the thousands. "I think the largest herd in the world roamed over the deep grasslands of Point Reyes," wrote an early settler. Though the local elk population was hunted to extinction, enough animals survived elsewhere to save the species.

Special Issue:
The Long Trail

EVER SINCE THE coastal greenbelt was completed, hikers have been captivated by the thought that one day they would be able to hoist packs at Aquatic Park (or at Fort Funston) and keep on trekking until they reached the farthest headlands of Point Reyes: all by trail: all on public lands. It is a walk of over fifty miles. And it can be done right now. Some of the trail links are old roads, but the pathway is there.

This is both a promise and a problem. Last year, more than fifteen million people came to this complex of parks. *Fifteen million.* A small proportion, granted, are hikers; but with numbers like that it doesn't take a large proportion to result in a back-country crowd surpassing any ever seen in America. How can we keep the long trail from being a dusty, eroded, polluted hikers' freeway: a dreary parody of what the walkers came for? This has happened already to trails much less heavily used.

There is no possibility of keeping the long walk a secret. But the park people hope to play it down initially. No single trail will be given the special label; traffic will be spread over a net of alternates. Gradually, moving up from the south, increasing use will be accommodated by well-laid-out hikers' camps, incessant trail maintenance, and a lot of ranger patrolling, especially where hikers pass close to sensitive municipal watershed lands.

MANY MAJOR NATIONAL parks have large concessionaires: suppliers of public services who are working for profit. It has been charged (most notably at Yosemite) that concessionaires unduly influence park policy. The Golden Gate greenbelt does not have this problem. But it does contain private operations of a different and much more sympathetic sort.

The Miwok Stables at the end of the Tennessee Valley Road, for example, have been there for years. Most of the horses belong to kids from nearby neighborhoods. There's just one problem: long-standing policy for the entire national park system forbids such tenants. Anything and everything inside a

Special Issue:
Changing the Rules

park, the rule goes, must be available to all. No service can be restricted to members of a particular club.

The principle, sound as it seems, may need a little bending in the greenbelt. For this park has a highly unusual connection with its users. For many people it is a familiar neighborhood. Special uses have grown up. And it may be unreasonably harsh to sever these because of a policy shaped for other kinds of situations. There is an important difference between encouraging such uses to develop—which would be foolish—and permitting established ones to remain.

The Miwok case is representative of others. Near Muir Beach is another private stable with a similar story—and with similar public support. And on the coast north of Muir Beach an environmental education center occupies a cluster of old houses. If it weren't there, one wouldn't want to put it there—this bit of coastline ought to be empty; yet the center is successful, popular, even loved.

It may be that a new kind of park requires some backing off from principle.

The Unprovided-for

"SOMEBODY'S GOING TO be left out in the cold," planning team co-leader Ron Treabess warned, "they won't be happy." But thanks to the sheer size of the park, not many interests *have* been left out. Still there are a few.

One group that has not gotten what it wanted is the recreational vehicle public: the people who travel in self-contained campers and trailers and who are accustomed to campgrounds with hookups for sewer-drainage and power. The staff initially suggested a site in Rodeo Valley, but so many people objected to the appearance of such an encampment in the austere surroundings of the Headlands that the idea was dropped. It doesn't appear that another site will be judged more suitable.

There is little in the park, either, for the auto camper—people who feel a need to back right into a campsite and have the ice chest on the tailgate. (Samuel Taylor State Park, adjoining the Olema Valley on the east, has this kind of space.) Instead, walk-in camps—you carry your gear a hundred yards or so—are to be provided.

Dirt-bikers and other off-road vehicle users have also made out poorly. Convinced that the general climate of opinion would not favor them, these users did not push their case very hard. A suggestion for a motorcycle trail the length of the park was not pursued.

These most notably excluded parties have something in common: their recreation depends on private motor vehicles. Though it was not applied deliberately, the principle behind the decisions is evident: that a given amount of land can handle a much larger population if users come by foot or hoof or pedal, or on public transportation. The policy that emerges is one of hospitality to people but not to their machines.

THE VANISHED TRIBES

THE WOMAN SITS on her haunches, weaving a basket. A dozen people watch her work — passing the colored rushes in and out, quickly, accurately; building something out of nothing. When she is done, the vessel will be watertight. She seems to forget that she is only an interpreter, imitating the skill of some dead Miwok Indian. "This," she tells us, "is the way we do it."

At Kule Loklo, a model Indian village constructed by ancient methods near the Bear Valley headquarters of Point Reyes National Seashore, rangers and volunteers illustrate the lives of the vanished people who occupied this land before whites came to it.

Their skin was copper-colored; their hair straight and black; their faces predominantly round. Shorter, on the average, than the whites, they had strong backs and powerful arms. They were tireless runners and could carry astonishing loads.

Hunters and gatherers, they depended on the yields of the land. Mussels and clams; salmon and venison; seal meat and bird meat and (occasionally) whale meat; berries; and the omnipresent acorn: these were their rich harvest. Though they had no true agriculture, the Miwoks practiced a sort of husbandry, setting fires to keep down brush and maintain forage.

Their population, small by our measures, was dense by Indian standards: several people per square mile. Their settlements clustered on the shores of estuaries. Many of their mounds are within the greenbelt, especially at Bolinas Lagoon and on the esteros of Point Reyes. Their huts were commonly thatched with reeds; they also had elaborate sweathouses and dance-houses. They built reed boats for travel on San Francisco Bay and may even have ventured into ocean waters. Their money consisted of clamshell disks, and it was important to them, personal wealth being highly valued. They feuded bloodily, family against family or tribelet against tribelet, but did not have large-scale war.

North of the Golden Gate were the Coast Miwoks; to the south lived the Costanoans. But "tribes," as such, hardly existed. The real unit was the local band or "tribelet." All spoke similar languages and belonged to the vast central California cultural complex. The special central Californian institution was the *Kuksu,* a

Marilyn Goudeau

secret society into which young men were initiated; its members carried out complex rituals of a religious and magical nature. The *Kuksu* practitioners were the only California Indians to use a form of drum.

The end of the Miwok era began in 1776 with the founding of the Mission San Francisco de Asís (known also as Mission Dolores). At first the "gentiles"—Indians—were not forced to convert, but after about 1800, whole populations were brought to the missions, and the countryside emptied. Mission San Rafael, built north of the Golden Gate in 1817, soon completed the gathering-in of the local tribes.

Life at the missions was by no means cruel, yet the Indians brought there did not do well. Disease reduced them steadily. Deaths always outnumbered births. For some reason the northern tribes declined more swiftly under this regime than did those nearer Mexico. Perhaps if mission life had gone on undisturbed, the Indian population would have recovered. Instead, in 1835 the new Mexican government secularized the missions—that is, closed them. Little provision was made for their unwilling dependents. Some Indians stayed on dejectedly at the sites; some found work on ranches; some tried to resume their old way of life. Lands that had been given to them were seized by settlers or bungled away. By 1848 the Indians of the Bay Area were reduced ninety percent. In 1920, according to one count, there were five living Coast Miwoks and about twenty Costanoans. A handful of people now claim descent from the tribes.

For years it was fashionable to shrug at the passing of this culture. "Too bad," was the attitude, "but is it really a loss?" Drake's men had reportedly admired the Indians, but the Americans, in particular, held them in contempt. Historian Gertrude Atherton called them "brainless": "so stupid that they rarely learned one another's language, so lethargic that they rarely fought. The squaws did what work was done; the bucks basked in the sun for eight months of the year, and during the brief winter sweated out their always negligible energies in the *temescals*." The Miwoks and the Costanoans, who indeed lived in something of a cultural backwater, were thought especially despicable.

But as anthropologists began serious study of the remnants of Indian culture, they repeatedly revised their opinions. Decade by decade, they have found more complexity and interest in the old society. Though the California Indians never passed beyond the hunting and gathering level, they are now thought to have built one of the most elaborate hunter-gatherer societies in the world. More and more elements are emerging which the "brainless" tribes were not supposed to possess: class systems, intriguing government mechanisms, alliances, highly developed rituals. These show no lack of ability. The specialists wonder: What prevented these people from making the seemingly slight step forward into true agriculture?

The California Indians of vanished tribes — Miwoks and Costanoans among them — need not be idealized or glamorized. But they deserve a far better place in memory than we have given them so far.

People to the Parks: The Transportation Problem

ONE ISSUE, MORE than any other, troubles the future of the Golden Gate greenbelt. That is the problem of transportation: the problem of getting people into the park and out again, smoothly, pleasantly, and cheaply, and doing so without tearing down the hills.

With the city's superb transit network, the San Francisco lands of the park ought to be very easy to reach without a car. Only modest changes and added services are needed.

The real problem is on the Marin County side. The parks in Marin have been called the recreational lung of the metropolitan region. They are lunglike, at least, in the way they suck in and expel the masses of weekend traffic. On many roads and streets in Marin and leading to Marin, the worst traffic jams no longer come during weekday commutes: they come on summer Saturdays and Sundays. The cars line up for miles on the tortuous roads over the hills to the sea, honking, braking, fuming. There is a kind of desperation in the push to get to the place where the fun begins. It certainly doesn't begin on the crowded road.

The fun is missing, too, for the neighbors: the people who live on the routes to the parks or actually within them: who sometimes find they have no place to leave their own cars, no safe way to cross Main Street, and no quiet. And the fun is missing for the people who don't drive or don't own cars—half the population of San Francisco and the East Bay cities—for whom Mount Tamalpais seems as far away as Mount McKinley.

IN THE OLD days the congestion problem puzzled no one. Traffic jams, according to simple wisdom, were a matter of "too many cars, too little concrete." The answer, always: pour more concrete. Such solutions were duly offered for West Marin.

In the 1960s it was thought that the region would follow other rural lands into a suburban future. The West Marin Master Plan of 1964 projected an ultimate population on the coast of 66,000. In aid of that plan, Marin's Board of Supervisors asked the state to build one of the several freeways the engineers had in mind. But in 1966 events took a new direction. At a hearing in Kentfield, ostensibly called to select the final route, a vociferous crowd insisted that *no* route made sense. "Freeways in this area," one coastal resident told the startled highway planners, "are insane and inane."

The state backed off.

A few years later the Board of Supervisors changed its viewpoint and resolved to maintain the western county as a mixture of parks and ranches. But the problem of weekend congestion remained.

In 1970 the county explored the thought of a new road designed for recreation only—the Bolinas Ridge Parkway. This highway would have left U.S. 101 at the Headlands and followed the coastal hilltops over Tamalpais (bisecting the tangle of roads already on the mountain) to the long north-trending summit of Bolinas Ridge. This it would have followed for miles, descending at last to the town of Point Reyes Station. But, in the anti-highway atmosphere of Marin County, the idea withered. Since then, any substantial change in the coastal roads—even the straightening of curves—has been protested.

In truth it is unlikely that more and better roads would have solved the problem. Congestion seems to follow the bulldozer as rain was once thought to follow the plow. And in the end the swelling traffic to West Marin would have exceeded the capacity of that most inflexible link in the chain of roads: the Golden Gate Bridge itself.

The Recreational Travel Study

WHEN CONGRESS CREATED the Golden Gate National Recreation Area in 1972 it also asked for a study of the transportation problem. This took place—an elaborate, expensive affair—and results were published in 1977.

Much of the money was spent to prepare sophisticated computer models of the traffic flow. These confirmed what everybody knew: that, unless a new course was entered, weekend traffic would keep the Golden Gate Bridge, the Coast Highway, and San Francisco's Marina Boulevard jammed from dawn till dusk.

The same research, however, yielded a conclusion less expected and a good deal more disturbing: that even an ambitious transit program would reduce the problem only by slight percentage points—unless and until the authorities began to discourage strongly the use of cars. Such measures are not pleasant, and the planners understandably shied away from them.

It follows, then, that the providers of transit to the parks must settle for limited goals. Clearly they have no hope of eliminating the congestion problem. But they do have hope of performing a second and scarcely less important job: to guarantee that people are not excluded from the public parks simply because they don't own automobiles.

THE PLAN THAT comes out of the transportation study is rather modest. It concentrates on making the park accessible to people without cars and promises only a small start toward the goal of freeing the park of its traffic snarl.

The Beginning

The plan would be carried out by three agencies working together: the San Francisco Municipal Railway; the Golden Gate Bridge, Highway and Transportation District (whose buses serve the Marin commuter); and the Park Service. The Service's contribution would probably be, not buses or drivers, but money to pay for added (and by nature unprofitable) routes.

From the transit point of view, the Golden Gate greenbelt has two broad zones. The southern zone includes the San Francisco rim and the Marin Headlands; the large and less accessible northern zone takes in Mount Tamalpais, the Olema Valley, and Point Reyes.

In the southern zone the San Francisco Municipal Railway would redesign some routes and schedules: minor changes to make the trip to the city's coastal parks quicker and more convenient. In addition the Park Service would subsidize several special recreational shuttles. The first, and most important, would carry people from Fort Mason headquarters west along the waterfront to the Golden Gate Bridge and across it into the Headlands, ending at popular Rodeo Beach. A second shuttle route, serving the same beach, would begin at East Fort Baker, a "visitor convergence point" with parking lots and ferry service. A third route, on the San Francisco side, would follow the ocean coast of the greenbelt from the bridge toll plaza past the Cliff House and south to Fort Funston.

Other shuttles would run on water. Ferries already serve Angel Island and Alcatraz; an East Fort Baker run would be added. Fort Mason would be the probable San Francisco landing. (The ferries have great advantages. They add nothing at all to the traffic on the seriously overcrowded Golden Gate Bridge and, best of all, they're fun. The water trip is not just a dull preliminary—it's an event.)

So much for the southern zone. The problem of providing transit to the remoter reaches of the greenbelt, from Mount Tamalpais north, is more difficult. Distances are longer, roads are winding and narrow. Under the emerging plan, the Golden Gate Bridge District would carry people to the mountain and, by an inland route, to the Bear Valley headquarters of Point Reyes National Seashore, near Point Reyes Station. (These services exist already in skeleton; to be useful they would need to be multiplied many times over: more buses, more often, from more places.)

From Bear Valley, special shuttle buses would head out in several directions—northwest to Drakes Beach, due west to Limantour Spit, or south to Bolinas Lagoon and the southern trailheads. Long-distance hikers could easily lay out their trips from bus stop to bus stop.

All the proposed new bus services together would cost (by Recreational Travel Study estimates) some $170,000 a year; another $100,000 would be budgeted each year for the ferries. There would be one large capital expense in addition: $300,000 for a ferry dock at East Fort Baker.

Clearing the Way

WITH SO LITTLE debate about what should be done, and so much agreement that it should be done quickly, one would have expected progress to be rapid. It wasn't. For a time, in fact, ground was being lost. Highly successful shuttle routes, set up as experiments during the travel study, lapsed, and the service provided by the bridge district grew steadily more meager. In the summer of 1978 it was scarcely possible to get to the Marin County parks by bus at all.

The hitch was in the bureaucracy. The Park Service proposed to spend only $35,000 in the first year of the program. But because this small amount was not in the basic park budget, a special request had to be made; and that request had to pass through the little-known yet immensely powerful federal agency called the Office of Management and Budget.

This office, called by some "the great god OMB," is a curious creature. It was set up with the laudable purpose of stopping wasteful and overlapping expenditures. Occasionally, however, its rules have an effect quite opposite to those purposes. It was thus in the case of the Golden Gate transit plan. For reasons that look quite sensible on paper, but only on paper, OMB forbade the Park Service to subsidize feeder buses operated by local transit agencies. If those agencies couldn't provide the service without subsidy, OMB ruled, then the Park Service must set up (at great expense) an independent bus line of its own.

There matters stuck. But finally Congress, concerned at the lack of public transportation throughout the national parks, intervened. A 1978 law (authored by Senator Harrison Williams of New Jersey) gave the secretary of the interior the authority to set up arrangements like the one proposed at Golden Gate. The Williams bill authorized $6 million for transit demonstration projects at Golden Gate and a number of other national parks.

It appears that the tangle is untangled. The buses should be rolling through the greenbelt soon.

130

NOBODY KNOWS JUST how well the new system will work, just how much it will accomplish. It would be unwise, however, to count on dramatic changes. Today about two percent of the visitors to these parks arrive by bus or ferry; the projections are that this proportion might increase to ten percent. The fact is that most people who can drive will continue to do so. And it is hard to blame them.

At its best, driving the roads of the greenbelt is a pleasure second only to the fun of hiking, riding, or cycling its trails. On a winter weekday it is exhilarating to drive over Tamalpais, or out to the long headlands of Point Reyes, or through the Olema Valley. The roads are empty through the green land.

Southside Road, Mount Tamalpais

Most people, of course, don't see these roads empty: they see them busy on some holiday weekend. But for most travelers—and especially for families with children or pets—the stop-and-go trip over Mount Tamalpais is still more attractive than the bus. Even people who argue for transit service can be found adding to the Sunday traffic jam. The planners summarize the prevailing attitude: "I want to drive there, but everyone else should take the bus."

The truth is simple: to most people the situation, despite its annoyances, is not intolerable. To say it is, is only a figure of speech—or perhaps a prediction.

Traffic jams have not kept many people away from the parks in the past. At some point, however, this will change. The travel study suggests that the weekend trip to the coast will eventually become so unpleasant that many people will stop trying to make it. As a result, the use of the West Marin parks could level off.

Some observers, alert to the danger of destructive over-use of fragile lands, see no harm in such an equilibrium. Park Service planners, though, feel that the West Marin parks can absorb more visitors than they are receiving today—provided that the added visitors do not bring cars with them. Bus passengers, they feel, should be welcome still.

The buses, however, will be caught in the traffic jams the cars create. Riders will be just as discouraged as drivers, just as likely to stay home next time. So the parks will serve the public less well than they should.

To prevent this situation from developing the Recreational Travel Study sketched—but only sketched—some further more drastic solutions. If these were carried out, transit service would be expanded much beyond its early level. New shuttles would run to previously transitless locations. The waters inside the Golden Gate would be busy with ferries. There might even be an ocean-going ferry from Fort Mason to Point Reyes. Visitors would be encouraged to park on the urban outskirts and take park transit for many additional miles. In the San Francisco portion of the park, an old railroad right-of-way would become a transitway on which park vehicles would have no competition from cars. A similar restricted route might be found through Marin—though nobody seems to see just where.

There's another whole aspect of the long-range plan, and this is less palatable to the driving public. It isn't enough to provide transit; in order to make a real change, further measures must be taken to discourage driving by making it inconvenient, expensive, or even illegal.

Even the early-stage plan calls for certain automobile restrictions. The first spot from which cars would be excluded, on busy weekends, would be Rodeo Valley in the Headlands. In the long-range plan, such closures would spread. The dead-end road to the summit of Mount Tamalpais would be for transit only. So might some of the roads on Point Reyes. Parking would be restricted and high fees would be charged. Parking regulations would be strictly enforced. These are what the trade calls "disincentives," and they are not easily sold to the motoring public. But they work, and in the long run they may be absolutely necessary.

If all this seems a little farfetched, consider that the lands now in the greenbelt once had an excellent transit system. It was fast. It was efficient. Millions used it. The excursion—ferry from San Francisco to Marin, train to the Tamalpais summit or the redwoods or the coast—was considered a lark. Often people took what was called the "triangle trip"—north to the forests of the Russian River country in Sonoma County, back south via the coast of Marin. It could be done in a day, not much more time than it would take by highway now.

We can't go back to those days. Too much has changed. But maybe we can learn something from the memory.

From W. W. Elliott, San Rafael Illustrated and Described, Showing Its Advantages for Homes *(Oakland and San Francisco, 1884).*

BATTLE OVER THE
JAMBOREE

AFTER 1972 THE history of the Golden Gate greenbelt, for the most part, runs smoothly. Some controversies have nonetheless occurred, and none was sharper than the debate, in the summer of 1978, over the Whole Earth Jamboree.

The Jamboree was a festival promoted by Stewart Brand, an environmental publicist. Ten years earlier he had founded the hip-environmental Whole Earth Catalog; now he wanted to throw a lavish anniversary party in its honor. The format was kaleidoscopic: distinguished speakers by the dozen (each limited to five minutes); novel games with parachutes and gigantic floating world-globes; booths; music; and aikido demonstrations. It was to last two days and draw (by early estimates) 10,000 people on each of them.

In short, a damn fine party!

Brand wanted to stage his event in the Marin Headlands. There is in the Headlands a site that has become traditional for large events: the abandoned rifle range not far from Rodeo Lagoon. Its several grassy levels make this a natural fairground. But this was not the spot Brand had in mind. He was determined to hold his Jamboree in another part of the Headlands, a branch of the Rodeo Valley known as the Gerbode Preserve.

Unlike the rifle range, this valley is not on a public road. The land is empty and exposed—is, as somebody said at a hearing, "foggy, windblown and beautiful." But the Gerbode Valley has more significance than that. It is in fact the first landscape you encounter in the greenbelt, moving north from the Golden Gate, that begins to strike you as remote, as almost wild. It is not surprising that decisions about its use would be difficult.

The thought of putting 10,000 people a day into this spot brought different reactions. Some friends of the park were horrified; others felt that an underutilized parkland was finally about to serve a proper function.

To Brand—and to his many influential supporters—this was an opportunity to bring a large public to an area purchased in the public's name. It was a chance to show people (urban people especially) the edge of untamed country. The rifle range, in its less natural surroundings, would not do. Besides, the rifle range had "bad karma," according to Brand.

The opponents—including conservationists Amy Meyer and Bob Young—saw a jamboree in the Gerbode Valley as a precedent for degradation. It would, they argued, drive away wildlife and dominate the view for miles of ridgetop trail. There was a question of fire danger. And one of precedent—would a pattern of such use be set? (Certainly Brand wished one to be set.)

The debate that followed was confused and sometimes bitter. Jamboree supporters portrayed the opponents as selfish exclusionists. "Whites, particularly from Marin, want to close the doors of the public lands behind them," one speaker charged before the Citizens' Advisory Commission to the Park Service. In the end a divided commission gave approval. Park Supervisor Lynn Thompson, emphasizing that no precedent was intended, told Brand to go ahead.

The opponents, however, were not finished. They turned to local authorities for help. After some vacillation, the fire chief of Marin County declared that a mass gathering in the Gerbode Valley would be highly dangerous unless elaborate precautions were taken. The county supervisors threatened to go to court unless the Jamboree was moved to the rifle range. Reluctantly, Thompson agreed.

And so, bad karma or not, the Whole Earth Jamboree took place on the rifle range. It was judged a splendid success.

Part 4

The National Debate

Parks to the People?

N O QUESTION ABOUT it—The Golden Gate National Recreation Area started something. Or maybe it would be better to say that a movement already stirring had its first confirming victory. It was not entirely new, this idea that there could be, near cities, parkland expanses large enough to measure by square miles. There were even a few precedents. In several areas, state or regional park authorities had put together splendid parcels. The federal government has been involved since 1962, when Cape Cod National Seashore and Point Reyes National Seashore got on the map. And with Indiana Dunes National Lakeshore, created in 1966, we had our first unmistakably city-linked national park.

But not until 1970 did the idea of a whole *system* of such parks emerge. It was Secretary of the Interior Walter J. Hickel who focused it. "Parks to the people!" he said, and soon proposed no fewer than fourteen of them: a pair, first, at New York and at San Francisco; then others at Hartford, Boston, Detroit, Chicago, Minneapolis-St. Paul, Atlanta, Memphis, Houston, St. Louis, Denver, Los Angeles and, at Washington, D.C., two separate areas. Not all of these were, in themselves, impressive projects; but together they made an impressive list.

The proposal imposed the thought that major metropolitan areas, wherever they were, should (almost as a matter of *right*) have great federal parks near them and linked to them. This thought was new. It was heady. It had power.

President Nixon's budget advisors sensed that power and were dismayed by it. They had no intention of spending on recreation the billions of dollars the program would have required. The president himself, up for reelection in 1972, gave enthusiastic backing to the first two National Recreation Areas, Golden Gate and Gateway; but soon after the election it was clear that the administration had no further interest in the matter.

It was too late, however, to stop the idea. Golden Gate, in particular, was a stunning precedent. Never before had so much money been spent to purchase so many privately owned acres so near a major city. The GGNRA became a prototype, a national example. The citizens of a hundred cities, distressed about the losses overtaking them, could look to this. According to one such conservation leader: "We have tended to identify with the GGNRA in San Francisco, with the hope that we might emulate its success."

Golden Gate:
First of the Many?

THE MOVEMENT FOR urban national parks has no secretariat, no central direction. It begins in the cities themselves. Local conservationists devise their own park plans and propagandize them. The national strategy consists of little more than a feeling that a given area is ripe for the push.

The first area to be ripe, after the initial pair, was one not even on Hickel's former list—the Cuyahoga Valley in Ohio. The Cuyahoga, a short gentle river, rises near the Pennsylvania line and flows to Lake Erie through Akron and Cleveland. It has a national reputation as a stream that did the impossible: in 1969, so thick was its coating of oil and pollutants, the Cuyahoga River in Cleveland *caught fire.*

But somewhat upstream, in the open land between Cleveland and Akron, the river is cleaner and runs in a broad green valley. This interurban lowland was threatened by the spreading suburbs of both cities. Regional park districts had done good work in acquiring parks in the valley but could do no more. The state had looked at the valley, considered the price of buying it, and backed away. In other words, the Cuyahoga was an utterly typical piece of privately owned metropolitan open space. It was pleasant; it was valued; it was needed; and it was in desperate trouble.

In Cleveland and Akron they'd heard the slogan "Parks to the People." So had local Congressman John F. Seiberling. Eastern legislators, he pointed out, had been voting millions of dollars for western parks for years. Now it was time for a little flow in the other direction. Late in 1974 Seiberling's bill for the Cuyahoga Valley National Recreation Area of 30,000 acres passed both Houses without one dissenting vote. A reluctant President Gerald Ford put his signature on the bill.

Then there came a hiatus. But in 1978 four additional national urban parks were created: the Chattahoochee River National Recreation Area north of Atlanta, Georgia; the Santa Monica Mountains National Recreation Area at Los Angeles; the Jean Lafitte National Historical Park in the swamps and bayous south of New Orleans; and, vaster than all the others combined, the million-acre Pinelands National Reserve in New Jersey. Of these more later.

Now that these projects, long in the planning, are cleared, we can expect to see new candidates. The backers of urban-area national parks have a list that includes most of the areas Hickel proposed, and quite a few more as well. Next targets: a Columbia Gorge NRA east of Portland, Oregon; and a Potomac River Shoreline Area upstream from the national capital.

A Change of Direction

*T*HUS THE MOVEMENT for urban parks accelerates. But even as it does so, its strategy is shifting. During the four blank years between 1974 and 1978, park advocates were confronting powerful critics; their approaches have changed as a result. Of the last four parks created, only one is comparable to Golden Gate or Cuyahoga.

The problem, not surprisingly, is money. The big close-in parks are magnificent; they are also exceedingly costly. Some people have been asking bluntly: "Are they worth it?"

The critics have charged that the National Recreation Areas, Golden Gate style, do not serve the people who face the most desperate shortage of recreational land—the urban poor and other people without cars.

They also argue that the big parks are not efficient as preservers of land. They cost too much and save too little. Only a handful of valuable and threatened landscapes can be saved by public purchase—the money simply isn't there.

And so an alternative program has been offered. To meet recreational needs, it would send more federal money directly to the inner cities for strictly local projects. To preserve natural or rural landscapes, it would put faith in a more modest but highly intriguing concept: that of the "greenline park" or "area of national concern." The notion, essentially, is to create "parks"—and that is not quite the right name—built partly of public land and partly of private land under unusually protective land-use controls.

In the face of this challenge, the backers of major parks have not abandoned their ambitions, but they seem to have modified them. They acknowledge (as indeed they always have) the need for a large investment in inner-city recreation. And though they still hope to see a lot of land put into public ownership, they are also convinced that the greenline park, or something very like it, will have to do much of the job of protecting close-in open land.

Let's look at the pressures that brought about this change, and at the national policy, still only half-defined, that seems to be emerging from them.

The Pressure of Expense

*S*IXTY-ONE MILLION DOLLARS to acquire the Golden Gate NRA; $40.5 million for the Cuyahoga Valley; a projected $155 million for the Santa

141

Monica Mountains. Compared to the amounts spent on water projects, for example, these are not huge sums; but they add up. It was estimated several years ago that the cost of twenty-three new National Recreation Areas near cities would be $5 billion. Today, no doubt, it would be much more. Land prices are rising so quickly that even modest purchases look forbiddingly expensive. And voters (thus also members of Congress) are no longer in a spending mood.

Yet the cost of acquisition is not the principal strain. (Looking back over the history of American parks, it is hard to find a purchase that was not regarded as extravagant when it was made—and impossible to find a case where the purchase was later regretted.)

The more troubling cost is the expense of developing and managing the property. Rangers by the dozen to meet the public and protect the land. Park police—a job recently invented—to protect the public from some of its own members. Planning staffs to spend long months in meetings and hearings. Transit systems—absolutely essential and, if done in earnest, terribly costly. Historic structures—numerous in parks near cities—to restore and save. The Golden Gate NRA and Point Reyes together have a long-term development budget of over $100 million; Gateway NRA in New York is allotted $300 million. Annual costs are approximately $7 million at Gateway, a little less for the San Francisco parks.

Nobody says this is money ill-spent. But if the list of urban-area national parks grew to twenty or thirty, the cost would indeed be daunting.

Some argue that we should be happy to pay the price: that a civilized nation should give its parks a bigger share of the budget. Maybe so. But such a transformation of priorities does not seem likely soon.

One thing is certain: if the Park Service acquires a "new tier of parks," as one advocate has called them, it could quite conceivably double its need for staff and money. To avoid neglecting the old-line natural parks (and they cannot stand much neglect), the Service would need a vastly enlarged budget. So far this has not happened. In fact the budget—measured either per visitor or per acre—has been steadily declining. And whatever happens in the field of urban parks, this trend toward degradation must be stopped.

Parks to the People:
A Lie?

FROM THE BEGINNING the big urban parks have been promoted in part as needed social services. Park supporters love to bring out figures showing the amount of open space their city has per capita (it is usually quite tiny). And they claim that their projects will bring special benefits to those who are most deprived. "Only a national park," said a proponent of the Santa Monica Mountains NRA, "can provide for real public access on a scale necessary to begin to meet the needs of the eight to ten million people in the Los Angeles metropolitan region. This huge new city is perceived differently by those who

A SHOPPING LIST
OF NATIONAL PARKS
NEAR CITIES

AT PRESENT THE Golden Gate greenbelt is a unique specimen. It may remain so: a sweep of public open space of such size, such beauty, and such integrity as to be beyond replication by another major metropolis. Yet it is not alone. It is a member, however outstanding, of a growing class.

At present there are eight federal greenbelt parks — major expanses, government owned or in the "greenline" style, that actually border on great cities. Soon there may be more.

Indiana Dunes National Lakeshore, Indiana. The oldest of the urban-area national parks. Twelve thousand acres of sand dunes and fascinating forest (wrapped around pockets of heavy industry); fourteen miles of shoreline on Lake Michigan. Twelve million people live within easy travel range.

Gateway National Recreation Area, New York and New Jersey. A cluster of separate parcels around the mouth of the Hudson River estuary; 27,000 acres in all. Gateway's greatest assets are its splendid sandspit beaches and its vast wetland, Jamaica Bay on Long Island: the only wildlife refuge on a subway line.

The Golden Gate National Recreation Area, California. With adjacent parklands, it creates a unit of some 120,000 acres, almost all contiguous: nearly two hundred square miles.

The Cuyahoga Valley National Recreation Area, Ohio. Thirty-one thousand acres near Cleveland. A gentle river-valley with bordering steep escarpments; rocky gorges; diverse forests. On the Ohio Turnpike. Five million people live within fifty miles.

Chattahoochee River National Recreation Area, Georgia. The Chattahoochee, "river of the flowered stones," flows from the southern Appalachians through the center of Atlanta. In 1978 it became the first great greenline park with federal involvement. About 7,500 acres, in scattered tracts, are to be publicly owned; a much larger area has land-use controls imposed by the Atlanta Regional Commission.

Santa Monica Mountains National Recreation Area, California. Alplike in profile, if not in height or vegetation, the Santa Monica Mountains rise almost at the center of Los Angeles and run west along the coast for fifty miles. Megalopolis surrounds their inland side. The new NRA contains some 70,000 acres of state and federal parkland.

Jean Lafitte National Historical Park, Louisiana. On the southern fringe of New Orleans, around brackish Lake Salvador. Twenty thousand acres of Delta forest, swamp, and marshland: headwaters of one of the most productive fish nurseries in North America.

Pinelands National Reserve, New Jersey. Between New York and Philadelphia: almost a million acres of pine, oak, sand dunes, and intricate waterways. This will be the principal testing-ground for the "greenline" concept: a quasi-park preserved by regulation.

Numerous landscapes have been suggested as possible future urban parks; as you read this, some may already have been so designated. Here are some candidates, and the cities they would be associated with:

New York. A "western metropolitan greenbelt" in northern New Jersey; also a "Suffolk County farmbelt" on Long Island—both greenline areas.

Boston, Massachusetts. A greenline park along the Charles River. Also a Boston Harbor Islands NRA.

Washington, D.C. A Potomac River Shoreline Area. Beginning near the Capitol, such a park could be 200 miles long. Would absorb the existing Cumberland and Ohio National Historic Park. The Anacostia River has also been suggested as a major urban park for the District.

Miami, Florida. Water and land around Biscayne Bay, incorporating an existing national monument.

Detroit, Michigan. A possible shoreline park between Detroit and Toledo, Ohio.

Chicago, Illinois. Twenty miles of shoreline on Lake Michigan, between Chicago and Milwaukee.

Minneapolis-St. Paul, Minnesota. An Upper Mississippi NRA threading between the two cities.

St. Louis, Missouri. A sizable area along the Meramec River.

Memphis, Tennessee. A Huck Finn NRA along the Mississippi.

New Orleans, Louisiana. The Pearl River, on the Louisiana-Mississippi line, could be the city's second close-in superpark.

Dallas-Fort Worth, Texas. The East and West Forks of the Trinity River have both been mentioned: the East Fork for its magnificent mixed forests, the West Fork for its location in the urban corridor.

Houston, Texas. Buffalo Bayou; also, a little farther out, the valley of the Brazos River.

Denver, Colorado. A Four Seasons NRA in foothill country between the city and the Front Range of the Rocky Mountains.

San Diego, California. Camp Pendleton, the vast Marine Corps base north of the city, is all that now separates expanding San Diego from the greater Los Angeles metropolis. Should Pendleton pass out of military use, it should certainly become a park.

Orange County, California. A possible park on remnants of the open Irvine Ranch coastline south of Los Angeles.

Oakland, California. Open ridgelines between Oakland and suburban valleys to the east; a possible greenline area.

Portland, Oregon. A Columbia Gorge NRA where the great river splits the Cascade Range. The eighty-mile park would run from rainforest on the outskirts of Portland to sagebrush desert east of the mountain chain. A lively campaign for this NRA is under way.

Seattle, Washington. A Puget Sound National Seashore has been discussed; so have parks along Hood Canal and the Nisqually River.

Buckeye

145

have automobiles, and those who are poor, young, old, and transit-dependent. It is the last who are the ones who need the park."

But *are* they?

In 1977 Congress asked the Park Service and the Bureau of Outdoor Recreation to make a joint study of recreational needs in major cities. Results came back in 1978. In most of the seventeen metropolitan areas considered, the situation was labeled intolerable. Typically there were shortages of recreational land for everyone; the closer you got to the center of the city, the greater the shortage became.

Did the writers see in this an argument for urban-area national parks? They did not. Quite the opposite: they believed that large parks on the urban fringe are all but useless to the inner city, that only parks in the center itself can serve the center. Big greenbelts may be gorgeous; they may contain urban sprawl; but, considered as recreational land, they serve the same suburban folk who are already best equipped with parks.

Adequate transit systems, one hopes, can help change this picture; but there is just enough truth in it to be troubling.

Instead of major new land purchases, the study suggested a massive program of grants to cities to help them rebuild and restore their old and run-down recreational areas. President Jimmy Carter endorsed this "Urban Park and Recreation Recovery Program" and Congress enacted it quickly, authorizing $725 million over a five-year period.

Inside the Green Line

SUCH REHABILITATION GRANTS do nothing to preserve close-in open space and natural areas. Now enters the thought of a land reserve of a new and relatively inexpensive kind: the so-called greenline park.

The term comes out of the Adirondack Mountains of New York. In 1892 the voters of that state, distressed at the logging of the upper Hudson watershed, amended their constitution to set up the six-million-acre New York State Forest Reserve. Within that vast zone the state would try to acquire private lands; whatever land it acquired could never again be logged: must be "forever wild." The boundary of that privileged forest was known, not as the green, but as the blue line.

The thought was that, sooner or later, the state would own most of that six million acres. It never came close. Today, New York owns only about two-fifths of the land inside the line. The remainder is private.

By the 1960s the Adirondacks had a bad case of what might be called "rural sprawl": that clutter of second homes, motels, shops, resorts, and gas stations, spreading along the miles of highways, that increasingly marks and mars even remote regions. One expert labels it "buckshot urbanization": a little of nothing much, everywhere. Local governments did nothing to slow this down; most of them had no zoning, no planning whatsoever.

What should be done? There was initial talk of consolidating the state lands into a new national park—thus essentially giving up on the other 3.7 million acres within the blue line. But this solution pleased no one. Instead, in 1971 the legislature created a special regional agency, the Adirondack Park Agency. Its job: to regulate the use of all land within the line.

Suddenly a lot of planning was going on where there had been none before; it was a shock. There was unhappiness. There were charges of socialism, arbitrariness, confiscation, harassment. There was bitterness. But (as has been the case elsewhere) the bad time passed. The courts, as they do routinely, upheld the planning power. Landowners realized that their basic rights had not been stripped away. And today the agency seems to be doing a reasonable job of keeping the mountains rural.

MEANWHILE, BACK IN Congress, the high cost of massive urban parks had begun to trouble the legislators. It especially bothered Senator J. Bennett Johnston of Louisiana, Chairman of the Subcommittee on Parks and Recreation, and his colleagues Harrison Williams and Clifford Case, of New Jersey. They turned for advice to the Congressional Research Service of the Library of Congress. In that office was a knowledgeable fellow, a specialist in environmental policy, named Charles E. Little.

What Charles E. Little Said

Little had been impressed by the example of the Adirondacks, still more by the national parks of the United Kingdom, which contain very little government-owned land. He pointed to these as a model for future preservation projects near American cities. Regions like the Santa Monica Mountains and the Pine Barrens of New Jersey should be protected, he argued, by buying just a fraction of the land and regulating use of the rest. Around such a complex one would draw, not a blue, but a green line. In comparison to traditional government-owned parks, Little saw several strong advantages in such preservation areas.

First, greenline parks are much less expensive per acre. The park agency—whatever its nature—can spend its acquisition money on special sites: lands of special natural interest; wildlife habitats; trail corridors; camping and picnic spots. It can also make its regulatory job easier by buying parcels where the pressure to develop is extreme. In other cases, it can buy partial rights to land. The bulk of the countryside—the setting—remains in private hands.

Second, such parks are less costly to manage. The landowners themselves are managers. Only certain portions are open to the public and are subject to the costs that this entails. (The Adirondack Park Agency, responsible for six million public and private acres, spends less than one million dollars a year.)

Third, greenline parks disturb local patterns of life much less than traditional parks do. A town like Bolinas in the Golden Gate greenbelt—

147

anxious above all to be left alone—might be happier in a greenline area than as an enclave in an expanse of public ownership.

Fourth, these parks can cover much larger areas than we could ever hope to buy outright—and can protect whole regions, whole ecosystems.

What Little proposed, accordingly, was a system of federal greenline parks on a vast scale. Every urbanized state, he wrote, might have four or five areas suitable for such treatment. In each case, a special agency would be established to prepare a plan for the greenline region. This plan would be reviewed by the secretary of the interior; on the secretary's approval, federal money would begin to flow. With one fund the National Park Service would buy the most important bits of private land; a second fund would subsidize the planning work of the regional agency. Every available tool, including density zoning and the purchase of scenic easements, would be used to protect the character of the landscape. If all went well, the Park Service could eventually transfer the newly acquired parcels to the local body.

Meanwhile, the many federal agencies that influence land use by the way they distribute money—grants for highways, housing, wastewater treatment, and so on—would take care not to make grants that would promote unwanted development within the green line. The greenline concept has been warmly endorsed by President Jimmy Carter and Secretary of the Interior Cecil Andrus.

But Will It Work?

CONSERVATIONISTS HAVE BEEN much attracted to the greenline concept. They have asked hard questions, however, about its details.

How can it be assured, once a greenline park is established, that the privately owned portions will continue to be protected adequately? How can it be assured—given the changing currents of state and local politics—that protection will be permanent?

A greenline park, if the federal government is involved, must be a partnership. The federal role, in essence, will be to provide needed money; the state and local role is above all to regulate land use, using powers the federal government lacks. Can such a partnership be kept from breaking down?

Greenline park advocates speak of cooperative effort and avoid talk of enforcement or pressure. But any such program must have guarantees. The obvious one is the power of the federal purse. Federal investment would be made contingent on state cooperation.

Some critics, both within and outside the government, doubt the force of this inducement. Once the money is spent, after all, it can hardly be taken back. One Park Service planner has remarked: "In order for the thing to work, you've got to have local commitment. In most places I wouldn't bet on it." The next few years plainly will be a time of both hope and testing.

CONGRESS, TOO, HAS had its doubts and debates on the subject of greenline parks. The uncertainty is reflected in the group of urban-area national parks created in 1978. Each can be seen as having two components: a traditional park at the core and, surrounding it, a greenline protective area of some sort. In each case a second look will be taken by Congress after a year or two of detailed planning. Each new park is an experiment, the results of which will be carefully watched.

The *Santa Monica Mountains National Recreation Area* will have a core area of some 70,000 acres of seashore and rugged chaparral-covered mountains. Another 150,000 acres—the balance of the range—are to be planned for by the Santa Monica Mountains Regional Commission. One hundred and twenty-five million dollars are authorized for land acquisition, an additional $30 million for grants in aid of state land-use management.

The *Jean Lafitte National Historical Park* at New Orleans will have an 8,000-acre core—the Barataria Marsh—and a 12,000-acre "park protection zone" in the marsh's watershed. State success in managing the zone will determine in part how much more the federal government invests in this park project. The secretary of the interior has stand-by authority to purchase land in the park protection zone.

The *Chattahoochee River National Recreation Area* north of Atlanta will contain 7,500 acres of public parkland in scattered parcels. Intervening lands are to be protected by an existing regional commission. Though the link between federal and state action is not explicit in the Chattahoochee legislation, it is understood that a land-use plan will be prepared.

The *Pinelands National Reserve* will be the most significant of all as a testing ground for future policy. Within its boundaries are almost a million acres of New Jersey's fascinating Pine Barrens, just south of the New York-Philadelphia urban corridor. There can be no question of acquiring any sizable percentage of this land. Twenty-six million dollars will be spent to acquire key parcels and subsidize planning by a state commission.

The establishment of these five areas in 1978 is due very largely to the work of one congressman, Representative Phillip Burton, head of the House Subcommittee on Parks and Recreation. Except for the Chattahoochee, all of the areas were included in Burton's dramatic Parks and Recreation Act of 1978—the bill known affectionately to many as the "Park Barrel."

THE CONCEPT OF greenline parks is like an optical illusion—like one of those drawings by M. C. Escher that contain two interlocking figures, black-on-white and white-on-black. Quite suddenly its meaning changes for you.

You can see a greenline area as a sort of weakened and extended park. It has figured thus in the present debate.

Or you can see it as a zone of strengthened land-use planning and control. This, I think, is its real and greater meaning.

A greenline park like the Adirondacks is nothing more and nothing less than an enclave of common sense. It is a line within which we agree to do, by special effort, what in fact we should be doing everywhere. And there is an assumption behind it—an observation, rather—that is galling: *Americans will ruin their country land unless there is a unique and compelling reason not to.*

But there is also hope—in more and more places we are finding reasons not to ruin. Many states, in fact, already have regions that resemble greenline parks, though they do not call them by that name. The entire coastline of California, regulated strictly by a special state commission, is such an area. San Francisco Bay can be considered a greenline park under the Bay Conservation and Development Commission. Florida's "areas of critical state concern," in which unusual protective standards apply, are similar. Some of these areas are more loosely regulated than the prototype Adirondack Park, and some more tightly; but the essence is the same.

Aware of this, perhaps, the Carter administration has coined a new term: Little's "greenline parks" are now known as "areas of national concern."

Seen thus, the greenlines can have double value. If successful, they will protect some valuable, vulnerable landscapes. But they may also serve as demonstration areas for the kind of land-use management we can expect to come to, sooner or later, by necessity, nationwide. Not incidentally, they may help to convince landowners that planning controls do not require major sacrifice—that, indeed, they can be to an owner's advantage.

Outside the Green Line

COMPARED TO THIS larger question—the organization of our use of land—the debate concerning greenline parks and standard parks is almost trivial. By federal intervention, however designed, we may keep some special places from being destroyed. But we should make no mistake: if we are unable to control the endless extension of cities, the cluttering of far-off countrysides, we will lose ten irreplaceable areas for every one we save.

For the moment, it must be admitted, parks are the one sure refuge we have from the spread of what Lewis Mumford has called "low-grade urban tissue." But it would be self-defeating to assume that this is the only option for the future.

In each metropolitan area we can decide, not tentatively but definitely, what lands will be developed and what lands—regardless of their ownership—will not. Once that decision is made, it is quite possible to hold the line. As in a greenline park, some of the open spaces can be purchased, some regulated, and some kept open by intermediate measures that may involve some payment. The tools are not perfect, but they are there. The courts, in most states, look with favor on their use.

In several states and many cities, attempts are being made to draw firm boundaries at which metropolis ends and countryside begins. In the San Francisco Bay Area, for instance, the citizens' lobby called People for Open Space is advancing a plan that would surround the bay cities with one great greenline park. One wishes them luck. In the region that produced the Golden Gate greenbelt, this is the next, and not less important, challenge.

MEANWHILE, THE DEBATE over short-term federal policy goes on. A balance is being sought among three lines of action.

The Three Tasks

The first, clearly, is to rebuild, clean up, and expand the recreational areas found within the cities themselves—the corner parks, the vacant lots, the playgrounds—and to build up the recreational programs that are just as necessary as the land.

The second action is to establish the greenline areas. That many will be created seems certain. There is good hope in them.

And the third line, still being pursued, is the purchase, for full public use, of major areas near major cities.

It is important that this idea not be abandoned. The greenline alternative should not become an excuse for turning down major traditional opportunities. Even in greenline parks there can be large areas of government-owned land; and even the largest traditional park could be strengthened by a greenline protective zone. There is no conflict between the two approaches. They are complements.

Better land-use controls (in whatever form they are packaged) could spare us the desperate, impractical compulsion to buy land wholesale simply to keep it open. But in many cases public acquisition is still wise. Though regulation and partial purchase can save many values, the fullest public use and the most total protection can only be achieved by public ownership. When there is a magnificent landscape in easy reach of the city, it ought to be added, if this is at all possible, to our permanent treasury of magnificent public places.

True, close-in public parks can't be considered the answer to general open-space problems; nor can they be counted on to meet urban recreational needs. They must be valued for what they contain, for what they are. Because they *are* near cities, such parks can provide something that neither playgrounds nor greenline areas nor distant areas usually can. That is contact: access: connection to what is wild.

To say that a scenic expanse a few miles from town is not much use to the inner city is to make an observation and also an assumption. The observation, easily made, is that the users of rural parks tend to have considerable income and education, and that they are disproportionately white. The assumption is that this pattern is somehow unchangeable.

Most conservationists would advance an opposite assumption: that the love of uncivilized and grandly scenic places is not merely cultural but is an intrinsic human absolute. Cultural differences or mere unfamiliarity may obscure this urge, or even kill it. But the predisposition is there.

I doubt that we can save these places — the wild, the odd, the remote, or the simply untroubled lands — unless the number of people who place high value on them grows vastly. These are fragile territories and fragile ideas. In an age of scarcity and short-term thinking, they always risk being set aside as luxuries. They are too vulnerable, politically, to depend for their survival on an elite — even on a very large elite.

In a place like the Golden Gate greenbelt, the door between the city and the wilderness is open. The whole range is there, from the landscaped city lawn to the forested arroyos of Point Reyes. With transit systems, with educational programs, with every means at hand, the promise of the greenbelt, its ability to captivate and teach, must be fulfilled.

And where we have other chances to achieve again what was achieved on the Golden Gate, we should do so.

For the sake of both the city and the wilderness, we need the wilderness next door.

WHAT YOU CAN DO

IS THERE, NEAR your own city, an extensive and undamaged landscape that you value—a landscape that your city, by its own expansion, seems likely to consume?

Do you feel impelled to do something about it?

If so, how do you go about it?

Here are some steps you might consider taking. "Steps" is perhaps the wrong word. These are things people find themselves doing when they set out to secure protection for some loved area of land. They are not invariable, nor need they follow a fixed order.

1. *Get information.* Find out what government agencies in your region make decisions about how land is used (city councils, planning commissions, county commissioners, boards of supervisors, freeholders, etc.). Start following their actions. Attend meetings. Learn what open lands are under development pressure, and how the local officials are responding. Form your own opinions. (Don't assume that development, simply because it is development, is bad.)

2. *Find friends.* Get in touch with people who share your interests, your worries. Find out what conservation groups are active in your area—go to some of their meetings. Listen to the instructive gossip that takes place when such people gather. Meet the people who can help you—or to whom you may give help. (You don't have to take a major part to have an influence.)

3. *Choose an issue.* Somewhere along the line (and often this is the first thing to happen, not the second or third) you will encounter some special case that captures your interest—a river valley, a coastline, a range of hills that seems unquestionably worth working to preserve.

4. *Organize.* If you've been working alone up to this point, find some allies! Get together and give yourselves a label: Friends of Big River, People for Green Mountain, or whatever. Even an exceptional leader needs colleagues in a job this size.

5. *Choose an approach.* Not every large piece of open land near a city is likely to become a National Recreation Area; not every such piece should. If a local government is doing a tolerably good job of protecting the land you're concerned with, you may need only to

offer your support. (Local officials who put limits on development inevitably must withstand a lot of pressure.)

If local policy is weak, you can set out to change it. If there are multicounty agencies that have some influence on land use—their nature varies greatly from state to state—you can turn to them. State government, too, may have an interest. Several states have policies for the protection of wetlands; a few are considering laws to protect prime agricultural lands.

What about buying the endangered land for parks or open space? Small areas may be within the budget of local governments; larger ones can be purchased by state agencies or special open-space districts.

When all these means seem insufficient, it's natural to look for help from the federal government. Such help should not be sought lightly. Ask yourself honestly: is the area that concerns you large enough, and special enough, to be worth a lot of federal money? Remember—you will have to sell the idea to skeptics.

If you plan to go for federal help, there is a further question. Should you advocate a National Recreation Area (something on the lines of the Golden Gate NRA)? Or should you opt for a "greenline" park, in which land-use regulation does most of the work? Actually, the two are not at all exclusive. Maybe the ideal would be a large NRA surrounded by a large greenline buffer zone—the sort of thing that exists in the Adirondacks. Or a small true park could be surrounded by a larger buffer. The combinations depend on the size of the area you're concerned with, the price of the land, and the moods of Congress.

6. *Build public support.* Take your idea to the public. Use news conferences, press releases, informal press contacts. Publish newsletters. Speak at meetings. When issues come up that concern your proposed park, take advantage of the resulting publicity to state your own case.

7. *Contact federal agencies.* Talk to the regional office of the National Park Service and the Heritage Conservation and Recreation Service (formerly the Bureau of Outdoor Recreation). Write the agency directors. Call attention to the area. Ask for a study.

8. *Contact representatives in Congress.* Get in touch with your two senators and your representative. Find out what they think. Don't insist on immediate backing from them; do insist on response. Even an unsympathetic legislator may be persuaded by signs of popular support. Keep letters coming in.

9. *Keep on plugging.* No matter what strategy you're using, success isn't likely to be quick. But it has a way of coming, after all, to those who don't stop pushing.

Index

Italicized numbers indicate illustrations.

The Author

Environmental issues have been the focus of JOHN HART's writing since 1970 when he began his career as a staff writer for the local *Pacific Sun*. He has since written two hiking guides for the Sierra Club, *Hiking the Bigfoot Country* and *Walking Softly in the Wilderness;* numerous articles for the local and national press; and in-depth reports for government agencies. Hart is also an accomplished poet: he won the Phelan Award for poetry in 1970; a collection of his poems, *The Climbers,* was published by the University of Pittsburgh Press in 1978. Hart was raised in Marin County. He now lives in the Sonoma County town of Healdsburg.

The Photographer

ROBERT SENA has an intimate knowledge of the Golden Gate parkland, as he was project manager of the consulting team that developed the master plan for the park. A landscape architect for the past ten years, Sena uses his talents as a photographer to record and interpret the land. His photographs have been exhibited in gallery shows in several major cities. Sena lives in San Francisco, where he pursues his dual career.

For information on the parks of
the Golden Gate greenbelt contact:

GGNRA Headquarters
Fort Mason, Building 201
San Francisco, California 94123
(415) 556-0560

Point Reyes National Seashore
Point Reyes, California 94956
(415) 663-1092

California Department of Parks and Recreation
Marin Area Headquarters
5710 Paradise Drive
Corte Madera, California 94925
(415) 924-9711